DESIGN and TECHNOLOGY

through Problem Solving

*A Resource Book for
Teachers in Junior
and Middle Schools*

Robert Johnsey

*Deputy Head
Reaside Middle School
Frankley*

SIMON & SCHUSTER

LONDON • SYDNEY • NEW YORK • TOKYO • SINGAPORE • TORONTO

Text ©Robert Johnsey 1990
Design and artwork © Simon & Schuster 1990
Photographs © Martyn Chillmaid 1990

First published in 1990 in Great Britain by
Simon & Schuster Ltd
Wolsey House, Wolsey Road
Hemel Hempstead HP2 4SS

Reprinted 1991

Printed and bound in Great Britain by
Richard Clay Ltd
Bungay, Suffolk

British Library Cataloguing in Publication Data

Johnsey, Robert
   Design and technology through problem solving
   1. Design and technology
   I. Title
   600
   ISBN 0–7501–0032–X

Photocopying

Editors: Julia Cousins and John Day

Illustrator: Jeff Edwards

Photographer: Martyn Chillmaid

Designer: DMD Ltd

Contents

**National Curriculum in Technology and
Science for Key Stages 2 and 3**
Attainment Targets 1 to 4 of the Technology
Curriculum are embedded in the activities
throughout this book, with an emphasis on the
processes and skills of designing, making and
evaluating a product. Also, each of Chapters 1, 3, 4
and 5 has a thrust towards Attainment Targets 6,
10 and 13 in the Science Curriculum. Chapter 2 is
focused on Attainment Target 6, and Chapter 6 on
Attainment Target 11.

To the staff and pupils at
Reaside Middle School, Frankley.
My thanks for your help
and encouragement.

Introduction

The work described in this book is based on the premise that children learn best when they are actively solving practical problems. If a child is intent on making an electric powered vehicle, she will more readily learn how to measure and cut materials, construct an electric circuit, work co-operatively with a partner and put the finished model through a test programme. She will need to exercise her powers of invention and be ready to analyse problems when they arise. Skills drawn from all areas of the curriculum might be included in a single integrated project but the most important aspect is that children will need to apply these skills in a meaningful situation. That situation might be related to a real-life problem, such as the need to design some climbing apparatus for the playground, or it may arise from an artificial challenge given by the teacher in which constraints are included similar to those of the rules in a game. There may not be an immediate need for a board game involving a marble following an obstacle course but children will enjoy being challenged to invent one.

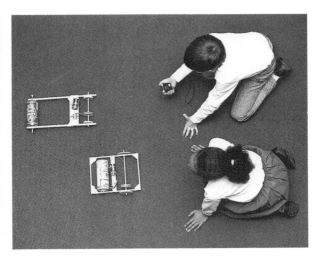

The problem-solving process

If children are truly to solve problems then they must be given decisions to make. Therefore, there must be elements of their work that are non-prescriptive so that they are encouraged to think for themselves. The projects described in the following chapters are based on a way of working which could be called the 'problem-solving process'. This is a description of the way in which many of us solve problems of an open-ended nature. Not all problems will be solved in this logical way, some solutions may be arrived at in a more random fashion. It is, however, a structure that we, as teachers, will find useful to have clear in our minds when we encourage children to solve practical problems. Elsewhere the steps involved might be described as the 'design process' but this only emphasises the close relationship between design and the kind of problem-solving described in this book.

Watering plants in the holidays

Suppose you encountered a problem concerning the watering of pot plants during the half-term break. The plants have been tended with care by the children but during the spring and summer months a week might be too long to leave them untended. You could take the plants home with you or you could ask the caretaker to keep an eye on them. You could give them an excess of water and hope it lasts (although experience tells you that this will harm many of them). Another alternative is to construct some kind of automatic watering system – a tap dripping on to the plants or a commercial stick that soaks up just enough water from a reservoir.

You might have time to read about some useful ideas in a magazine or you may have been lucky enough to have seen a recent television programme that has discussed the problem.

Finally, you take the advice of a neighbour and place the plants on a thick damp towel that can draw water from a bowl nearby. You take the precaution of trying this system for a few weeks before the half term so that you can be sure it works. As a result of these trials, you find the best position to place the bowl is slightly higher than the level of the plant pots. This allows sufficient water to soak into the towel.

The problem-solving process began with the definition of the need to keep the plants moist during a prolonged period. A number of solutions were considered and some investigations were made as to the best way to solve the problem. Once a probable solution had been chosen, the system had to be constructed and put on trial. The improvements as a result of these trials led to a satisfactory watering system.

The process that we have described looks like this:

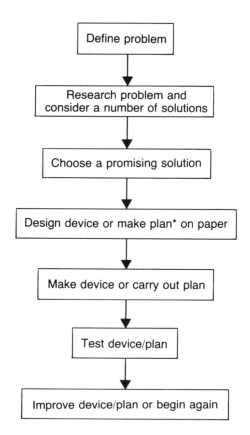

```
┌─────────────────────────┐
│     Define problem      │
└─────────────────────────┘
            │
            ▼
┌─────────────────────────────┐
│   Research problem and      │
│ consider a number of solutions │
└─────────────────────────────┘
            │
            ▼
┌─────────────────────────────┐
│  Choose a promising solution │
└─────────────────────────────┘
            │
            ▼
┌─────────────────────────────────┐
│ Design device or make plan* on paper │
└─────────────────────────────────┘
            │
            ▼
┌─────────────────────────────┐
│ Make device or carry out plan │
└─────────────────────────────┘
            │
            ▼
┌─────────────────────────┐
│    Test device/plan     │
└─────────────────────────┘
            │
            ▼
┌─────────────────────────────────┐
│ Improve device/plan or begin again │
└─────────────────────────────────┘
```

[*Not all problems require a device to be built, some need a plan to be put into action.]

The importance of research

Children solve problems by using ideas and skills that they already possess and re-mixing them in novel ways. If, however, they are presented with a problem for which they have insufficient previous knowledge, then their solutions will be either non-existent or fairly unimaginative. We can overcome this difficulty in two ways:

● We choose problems which have solutions that are already within the children's range of experience

or

● We provide the children with a variety of ideas and skills which they may use to solve the problem in hand.

This preliminary research phase will be most effective if the children already know the

problem they are being asked to solve. With a clear target in sight, children will learn more readily.

The research can be closely controlled by the teacher by the use of workcards or verbal instruction. Alternatively, more experienced children may be able to plan and execute their own preliminary work. Useful information can be obtained from books, video programmes, wall charts, slides or 'experts' in a particular field. The 'expert' might be another teacher, a neighbour, or perhaps a child in the same class who has some specialist knowledge such as kite building or fabric work.

Perhaps the best form of research is a practical investigation carried out by the child herself. This might involve a scientific investigation into the effect of gears or the position of the centre of gravity of an object. Perhaps making a simple model that partially works in card or other easily worked materials will be a necessary preliminary to modelling in tougher, resistant materials such as wood or plastic.

Part of this initial thinking period might include a discussion within the class as a whole or within smaller working groups. It might include a brainstorming session in which 'anything goes'. This can be good fun and highly informative. It is up to the teacher here to introduce a light-hearted element, encouraging humorous suggestions that, surprisingly, can sometimes lead to workable ideas.

Another part of this preparation phase might include learning how to use specialist tools such as a tenon saw or a pair of pliers.

Finally, the time spent on research is valuable in giving children a chance to decide how they will fulfil the particular brief they have been given. A true consideration of the problem is therefore achieved, thereby leading to a higher quality solution.

Designing on paper

When a suitable solution has been chosen in response to a problem, the details will then need to be worked out. If the solution requires the construction of a model, then a drawing of the proposed model will probably be needed, although this is not always essential.

The drawing stage gives children a little more time to think before they have to handle materials and tools. It is an excellent way to communicate difficult ideas to the teacher and vice versa. Children may have an overall idea for their model but may not have thought out essential details that can now be inserted on their plan. Improvements to a first idea can quickly be made on a drawing – a better shape here, a stronger bracket there – and a final colour scheme can be planned in advance.

For the teacher dealing with a large number of children, the design drawing stage can be an invaluable aid to classroom organisation. Children will finish their drawings at different times and be ready for construction. A staggered start to this difficult phase in the

project will prove beneficial to all concerned.

Inexperienced children may find it difficult first to imagine the model they are going to construct and secondly to place a two dimensional representation of it on paper. At first we won't expect all the detail to be there. We won't insist on accuracy of scale or shape, though we might expect accurate labelling and neatness. We can expect the use of a sharp pencil and ruler when necessary and the thoughtful use of colour where appropriate. The projects in this book describe a possible progression in graphic skills that are summarised below.

A progression in graphic skills

Simple drawing of simple models that might be cut out of card. Labels and colour might be added.

Simple side-view drawings of three dimensional models.

Drawings requiring straight edges and/or circles drawn with instruments.

Simple plan drawings – not to scale.

Plan and side-view drawings – not to scale.

Drawings including end-views.

Drawings exactly full size.

Drawings to a simple scale.

Perspective drawings of simple models.

Isometric or orthographic projections of simple objects.

Multiple drawings showing fine detail and working parts of a model.

Methods of shading and tinting drawings can be developed alongside the stages above.

Not all models have to be planned on paper beforehand. Sometimes a spontaneous response to a problem is desirable, especially if the model is simple and easily altered if improvements need to be made.

Sometimes, especially with younger children, a simple card model that perhaps partly functions can provide a much more realistic design plan than a two-dimensional representation. In Chapter 4, which involves the positioning of levers in a model, the technical details are first worked out with card and paper fasteners.

Design for a folding chair Scale 1:5

Introduction

The design drawing stage, then, is a time for communicating ideas and making important decisions. The skills used will be drawn from previous lessons in maths, art and science, and the finished drawing will prove to be invaluable as construction proceeds and points of detail need to be discussed.

Making

Some models can be made with classroom materials such as card and paper, but the scope of such work is greatly increased if resistant materials such as softwood, plastics and wire can be manipulated with simple tools. A special workshop is not necessary – though it does help – and the tools need not be expensive ones.

Materials

When children solve problems, one of the major decisions that they make will be which materials to use in construction. There are times when they should have a completely open choice of all the materials available to them, while at other times they may benefit from having a more limited choice. The list of materials that you offer the children will depend on the resources available at your school, the tools available to work them, and sometimes the constraints that you choose to impose on the situation. Another important factor will be the children's expertise in handling the materials and the safety considerations that are associated with this.

Below is a list of materials that could be made available to children beginning work in design and technology. Those items towards the end of the list should be introduced as the children gain more expertise. The nature of the following materials is discussed more fully in the appropriate chapters.

Materials that can be manipulated easily in the classroom

Paper of various qualities
Card of various thicknesses
PVA medium or similar adhesive
Sticky tape
String and thread
Paperclips
Paper fasteners
Drawing pins
Elastic bands
Thin plastic from containers
Fabrics
Modelling clay

Materials needing more specialist tools

Thicker plastics
Wire of various thicknesses
Balsa wood
Softwoods
Hardboard
Dowel rod of various diameters
Plywood of various thicknesses
Blockboard
Chipboard
Hardwoods
Metal fittings: screws
nails
springs
hinges
nuts and bolts
eye hooks

Tools, facilities and related skills

Throughout the projects described here, tools and related skills are introduced in a structured way. Specialist tools, such as craft knives and hand drills, can involve an element of danger if used wrongly by over-excited children. In the author's experience, children are adept at self-preservation and usually avoid hurting themselves even if they are using the tools incorrectly. They can, however, become frustrated if the job of cutting or shaping becomes laborious because they are using the tools inefficiently. They need a great deal of help initially while they learn to handle the tools, so a planned introduction through demonstration and practice exercises is important.

If you have never used some of the tools before, then read the sections marked with a labelled marginal rule in the relevant chapter and have a short practice yourself before teaching the children. There is nothing mystical about the skills involved in using any of the tools. They can all be mastered by an adult in a very short time.

You will already be familiar with a number of the tools in the following list. It is a good idea to consider introducing them approximately in the order shown.

Tools and facilities	Related skills
Pencil, ruler, compasses etc	Drawing straight and curved lines, measuring length, etc.
Scissors	Cutting and scoring
Hole punch	
Stapler	
Craft knife	Cutting safely
Pliers	Shaping wire, cutting wire
Hot glue gun	

Tools for wood

Tools and facilities	Related skills
Woodwork bench or protected table	
Woodwork vice (permanent or removable)	
Bench hook	
G-cramp	
Tenon saw	Sawing wood and plastics
Junior hacksaw	
Surform plane	Shaping wood
Rasps and files	
Glasspaper with block	
Coping saw	Cutting curves in wood
Drills	Drilling holes
Metalwork vice	
Hammer	Nailing wood
Screwdriver	Screwing into wood
Electric sander	Safe use of power tools
Electric bandsaw	
Electric jigsaw	
Electric pedestal drill	

The last four items on the list are not essential for the projects in this book, though children can be taught how to use them and they can also save time when used by the teacher to prepare wood suitable for the children's use.

The tools listed above could be obtained by a school over a period of years as a design and technology scheme is developed. The number of individual tools need not match the number of pupils in the group, as the same tool will not be used simultaneously by everyone.

More is said about the introduction of tools and related skills in the following chapters.

Testing and improving the model

When the model or device has been made, the children will need to see if it solves the original problem. This is where the children's sense of a fair scientific test will come into play.

Much will depend on the nature of the model. If it is a propeller driven vehicle, will it travel the distance specified? If it is a scale model of a folding chair, does it fold successfully? Does it look good enough to fit in the lounge and will it hold the kilogram mass without collapsing? We might expect an objective, scientific test for an invented burglar alarm but a more subjective assessment for a decorative balancing toy.

Faults and failures

The faults in the model will need to be analysed and corrected if possible. It should be made clear to the children that the process of solving problems is a never-ending one. Even a simple device like a can opener has room for improvement, demonstrated by the latest 'modifications' available on the market today. Initial failure is an important, even necessary, part of solving problems. However, children who have suffered due to failure in the past will need extra encouragement when it happens now. It often helps them if they see that their teacher is also sometimes at a loss as to the best course of action. One of the author's favourite ploys in such a situation is to scratch his head and say: 'I'm afraid I don't know what to do either but I'm sure there must be some way round the problem. What do you think?'

Part of our job in teaching children to solve problems is to engineer situations in which they can gain confidence in their abilities. While failure is often necessary in the problem-solving process, it should eventually lead to some form of success. This is not easy in a group of mixed-ability children, but it can be achieved by employing a number of strategies:

- Choose a problem that suits the interests and abilities of the children in your particular group. It will have to be a sufficiently open-ended problem to allow for solutions of varying sophistication.

- Be ready to give extra attention to those less proficient members of the group while at the same time prompting the more able children to stretch their powers of inventiveness.

- Children learn a lot from each other, so while you should encourage them to be original in their work it might be appropriate to allow some children to copy parts of ideas from others.

- Suggest some research that the children could do which will provide hints on possible solutions. Group discussions will also help here.

Finally, although we will spend much of our time trying not to give solutions to the problem, there comes a time when it is appropriate to spell out a clear answer to an ailing child. We do this in the hope that in the future the child will have gained the confidence to make decisions for himself or herself.

Safety

If children are to extend their skills by using the materials and tools listed earlier, they will have to be made aware of any special safety procedures that they should follow. In the following chapters a △ will appear in the margin when special attention should be given to safety. The triangle will contain a number that can be found on pages 93 and 94, where the corresponding safety procedure is described. In many cases it is a matter of reminding children that commonsense should prevail when using cutting tools and being prepared to cope with minor cuts and abrasions should they happen. The following specific points must be emphasised to the children:

- Keep loose clothing and long hair away from the tools.

- Follow instructions for the safe use of tools.

- Secure materials that are to be cut or drilled to the bench or table.

- Give yourself room to work, away from others.

- Keep body and clothes away from all cutting edges. Always assume that the blade might slip.

- Do not interfere with someone else's cutting job. They may not know your fingers are in the way.

• Keep eyes away from particles that are being scattered such as sawdust and wood chips. Wear safety goggles, if necessary.

• Take a rest from using tools if you are tired.

• Do not use a tool you are unfamiliar with until you have been shown how to use it correctly.

• Carry tools and materials round the room carefully. Never run.

• Know what to do if there is an accident.

If you have electric tools in use in your school the manufacturer's instructions regarding safety must be followed exactly. If children are to use powered tools they will have to be given clear instruction in how to use them and should be supervised for the first few times. Always use plugs or connectors with circuit breakers.

General organisation

The work described in this book has been designed so that it can be carried out in a variety of situations ranging from a small group of children in a classroom working an integrated day to a large group of 15 to 20 during a set time each week. It has been assumed, however, there will be time to discuss the project with the children at the beginning of the work and to monitor their progress regularly.

For some of the projects described later in the book, a work table or bench fitted with a vice will be essential. Some consideration will also have to be given to the safe storage of tools and materials. For a small group, tools could be stored on a trolley or in a portable box. If more tools are to be used, then a permanent cupboard becomes useful. Hooks or trays that are clearly labelled enable children to find and the correct tool and return it to its correct place. They also allow a quick check to be made on numbers at the end of the day. The children should be trained to collect tools and materials themselves so that the teacher can concentrate on discussing problems with groups or individuals.

How should I use this book?

Each chapter of this book represents a project that might last for half a term working at a rate of approximately two hours a week. The projects increase in their sophistication and their demand on resources and pupils' skills. While the ideas in each project could be taken in isolation, the eight chapters were originally designed as a scheme for junior/middle school children. Care should therefore be taken to ensure that children have acquired enough skill and experience to cope with the new ideas in a particular project if they have not already worked through the projects described in previous chapters.

There is a summary for quick reference at the beginning of each chapter, which includes the design task and the stages that the children will probably work through.

Sometimes it is appropriate to consider the science and technology relevant to each project in more detail. This is the function of a special section called About . . . , to be found near the end of each chapter.

In some instances teachers might like to use the principles involved in a project in a different situation. With this in mind, additional tasks are described in a section entitled Similar Projects at the end of each chapter.

1 Balancing models

SUMMARY

The task
Design and make a toy or ornament that is interesting because it balances in an unusual way on the edge of a table, on a small platform or on a short tightrope.

The first project is about designing and making models or toys that balance in an unusual way. Children will require little in the way of previous experience with tools other than scissors, craft knives, rulers and pencils. However, the use of wire, and therefore pliers to shape and cut it, may be new to them so this skill will need to be introduced at the appropriate time. The activity can take place in an ordinary classroom without any special work surfaces, so it makes an ideal introduction for those children just beginning their experiences in design and technology.

Introducing the topic

It may be possible to arrange the work as an extension to a current classroom theme. The ideas of balance and centre of gravity occur in many novelty toys, and in activities such as physical education and playground games. Scientific investigations may have included work on the stability of boats, double-deck buses or racing cars. The children may have recently visited a circus or have seen one on television. If they have watched the tightrope act or balancing clowns then these experiences will provide an excellent starting point for the following investigations.

In the absence of any of the stimuli mentioned above, try beginning the lesson by

- Asking someone to come to the front of the class and stand on one leg for as long as possible. How does she keep her balance?

- Placing a long block of wood, about 10 cm by 10 cm in section, on the floor. Ask a volunteer to walk along this without falling off.

- Placing some house bricks as stepping stones across the classroom. Ask a child to step across the room without falling off the bricks

- Asking children how they would cross a stream on a narrow log. Can they demonstrate on the block of wood?

In practically all situations where a human being has to keep his/her balance, the arms (and any other spare limbs) are used to maintain the correct position. A tightrope walker sometimes uses a long pole to emphasise this effect. Many animals use their four legs for support and their tail for balance.

Children may also know that if they crouch down low on a narrow log as they cross a stream, they are in a safer position than if they stand up. It is this idea of lowering the centre of gravity that they will come to appreciate as they progress through this project.

Setting a preliminary task

It would be a good idea at this stage to set the children an initial research project before they progress to the main task of designing and making their balancing model. Give the children the following instructions:

Use the template provided to cut out a figure from card. Then use the piece of flexible wire and Plasticine you have been given to make the figure balance in an upright position on the tightrope. You can use a small piece of sticky tape but you must not stick the model to the string in any way.

Figure 1 Suitable template

The children will need access to a model tightrope in order to solve this problem, so arrange for one or two to be set up around the room. This can be conveniently achieved by turning a desk upside down and running a length of string around its legs. A suitable template for making a card figure is shown in figure 1. Notice the notch in the foot of the figure. This will make the figure fit neatly on the tightrope and prevent its slipping off.

Green, plastic-coated gardener's wire is very useful for this exercise since it is both flexible and easily cut by young hands. A length of about 30 cm will be suitable for each model. The wire could be cut with a strong pair of scissors. However, this would be a good opportunity to introduce to the children the use

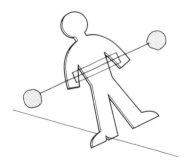

Figure 2 Impractical solution

of pliers for cutting wire, if they haven't already used them.

Depending on the children's previous experience, they may begin with some fairly impractical ideas such as the one shown in figure 2. This solution is akin to the circus tightrope walker and her pole. The children may wonder why she falls off the rope! Someone is also sure to discover the solution shown in figure 3. This is getting close to a workable solution but, unfortunately, the figure must stand *upright*, with its foot on the rope.

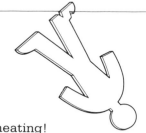

Figure 3 Cheating!

Why does the upside-down figure not fall off?

Where is most of its weight?

With a mixture of hints and persuasion, as well as learning from each other, the children will find a solution that works in a similar way to those shown in figure. 4.

Figure 4 Contrasting solutions

How much should I help the children?

Naturally the outcome of such an exercise will be unpredictable. The teacher needs to accept this and not become over-anxious about it. If children are truly to solve problems, then it won't help to tell them the answers. On the other hand, if the children become bored or frustrated because the problem is beyond them then, again, we have achieved nothing. Setting problems is itself like walking a tightrope. Hopefully our knowledge of the individual child should enable us to give a little information when necessary but also to withhold that help when it is appropriate. A lot of the work we do with children involves them following instructions, so they are used to asking for help. What we must get used to once in a while is refusing to give it!

During the tightrope problem you will have taken the opportunity to discuss with the children the idea that a low centre of gravity gives a body more stability. To be more specific: when the centre of gravity of a body is either over or below its point of support, the body can stand or hang there without falling. Give the children a chance to put these ideas into their own words at the end of the problem-solving exercise.

Moving on to the main task

Once the children have had a taste of solving a practical design problem, they will be ready to use the ideas they have learnt in a more substantial project. They may have realised that the balancing tightrope walker could be made into an attractive toy or ornament if it were made of more durable materials.

THE TASK
Design and make a toy or ornament that is interesting because it balances in an unusual way on the edge of a table, on a small platform, or on a short tightrope.

Explain to the children that before thinking too hard about their model they should carry out some more research into how shapes balance. This will help them to make decisions about their final model.

The worksheet opposite can be used as a suitable guide for the children to start their investigations. Whilst working through this sheet they will experience the following ideas which can then be reinforced by the teacher:

- A model can be made to balance on the edge of a table, on a platform or on a tightrope.

- The centre of gravity of the model needs to be under the point of support for the model to balance.

- If the wire is bent into a suitable shape, the part above the the table can be made to stand upright.

- The model can be made to rock to and fro.

- The further the weight is below the point of support, the slower it rocks. (This is similar to the way in which a pendulum works.)

- The model can swing around the point of support, which could be a finger or a cork in a bottle.

- If the weight is too small the model will fall or tilt.

- The card can be cut to any shape as long as it goes around the table edge and supports a weight under it.

Discussing the model design

Make it clear to the children that they are now going to design a model of their own. It will have a weight attached at the bottom that will come below the support surface and it may rock or swing around. Tell them not to choose one idea now but to suggest lots of ideas that perhaps their friends could use.

What could the model be?

Balancing clown
Rocking horse
Spinning dancer
Boat at sea
Bird sitting on the edge of a table
Monkey swinging from the edge of a table
Spinning roundabout

Encourage the children to think of an idea of their own that is quite different from anyone else's.

What materials can be used?

The children will only be using materials that can be shaped in the classroom with the usual tools such as scissors, craft knives and pliers.

Worksheet

Balancing Act

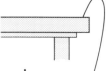

1 Bend some wire into this shape exactly. Check the shape of your bent wire by laying it on here.

2 Can you make it stand on the desk like this?

Does it twist under the desk?

3 Make it stand up by fixing some Plasticine somewhere along the wire.

4 Experiment to find the smallest amount of Plasticine that will make the wire balance correctly on the table.

5 Bend the wire into different shapes to make it balance.

More Balancing

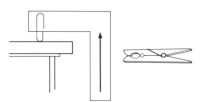

1 Cut out a piece of card like this.

Draw an arrow on it.

Fix a paperclip to it.

2 Put a clothes peg anywhere to make the card balance on the edge of the table. Make the arrow point straight upwards.

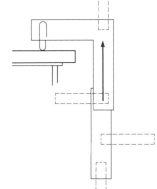

3 Make the card longer as shown. Then make the arrow point straight upwards, again using the peg.

4 Cut out some different shaped pieces of card and try to make these balance on the edge of the table using clothes pegs or Plasticine.

Do they swing in different ways?

Balancing models

There are limitations as to how these materials can be fixed together. PVA adhesive is suitable for card, paper and wood but not for wire and plastic. In some instances these can be stapled together, or the wire can be twisted into position. A hot glue gun will overcome most joining problems.

Some suitable materials that can be used are shown in figure 5. They will probably include:

Wire – florists wire, welding wire, coathangers
Plastic – polystyrene, discarded bottles
Fabrics
Paper and card of various thicknesses
Corrugated card

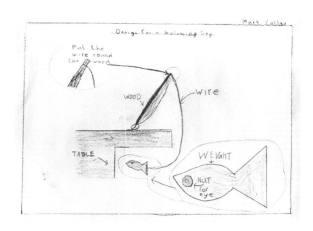

Figure 5 **Suitable materials**

The weight at the bottom of the model could be made from Plasticine. However, this is likely to fall off, so some pre-cut pieces of hardwood with small holes drilled in them for wire to be passed through are recommended. Another solution would be to make a saw cut in a block of wood; this enables the end of a card model to be glued into position. Alternatively, provide some large fishing line weights or hexagonal nuts.

Drawing the design

When the children have had enough time to consider possible models and the materials that they could use, it will be time for them to design a model of their choice. Ask them to make a drawing of their ideas. This will probably be very simple and informal at this stage in their development, but it will be all right as long as it portrays the basic features of

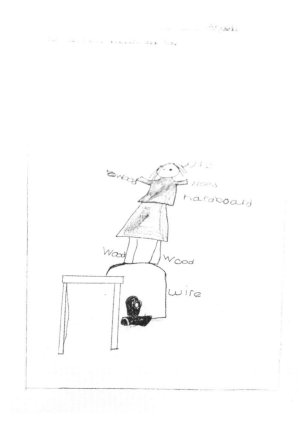

Figure 6 **Contrasting proposals**

their design. However, it might be worth asking them to decide on a colour scheme for their model and transfer this to their drawing using coloured pens, as well as labelling the types of material they intend to use and how they will fix them together. The actual drawing should be as large as the page will allow rather than tucked away to one side. If you can provide large enough sheets of paper you could ask for a full-sized drawing of the model.

While the children make their drawings you

could use the time to help the less imaginative and discuss impractical details with the over-ambitious. Take the opportunity to broaden the children's vocabulary while discussing their work. You will probably need to sort out any misunderstandings that have arisen over the nature of the design brief.

The following typical situations will help to illustrate some of the issues that could arise during this project.

Sally's parrot

Sally had drawn a parrot with a long curved tail. The feet rested on the table while the weight was fixed to the end of the tail. Her experience told her that she could cut the parrot out of a flat piece of card.

'Do you want to make a flat parrot, or a solid one?' asked her teacher.

Sally replied that she would really like to make a solid one, but that she didn't know how to do it.

'Tell me something that is thicker than card,' said her teacher.

Sally thought, and then suggested, 'Wood?'

'Go on, there must be lots of other ideas,' prompted her teacher.

Sally's friend was encouraged to join in to give Sally moral support.

'You could use lots of pieces of corrugated card and glue them all together,' Dalvinder suggested.

With their teacher's encouragement the two girls came up with even more ideas: two pieces of card glued to each side of a small block of wood; a single piece of card with thick fabric glued to each side; papier mâché. Their teacher added the idea of cutting the bird shape from a shampoo bottle thus giving a solid effect.

Sally eventually decided to cover a piece of card with thick, fluffy fabric to make her parrot. She and her friend, however, had learnt the benefits of pausing to consider a number of solutions to a problem before attempting the 'final' solution.

John and Mark's roundabout

John and Mark had chosen to work together. They were intrigued by the way the wire in the research exercise had swivelled around when balanced on a finger tip. This had given them the idea of making a roundabout which could rotate on the top of a plastic lemonade bottle. Figure 7 shows what their drawing looked like.

It wasn't clear from the boys' diagram how the roundabout would be made so their teacher made a point of discussing it with them. The roundabout was apparently made of 'pencil lines'. Their diagram didn't show how the parts would be fixed together or how the roundabout would balance. The boys also seemed to have missed the point about lowering the centre of gravity since the whole of the model was above the point of support.

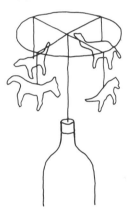

Figure 7 John and Mark's roundabout

Their teacher decided to deal with the problem of balance first. She took one of the models of the card tightrope walker and asked what would happen if the Plasticine weight was positioned above the tightrope. Once the model had fallen off the rope the boys could see more clearly what was wrong with their drawing. They realised that the shapes on the roundabout would have to be made as heavy as possible and positioned as low as possible.

They hadn't at first considered the way in which their wire model would be fixed together but during discussion with their teacher they decided to neatly fix the wires with sticky tape.

Sabrina's mouth

Sabrina was an imaginative girl who was keen to try something different. Her drawing showed a large head which appeared to be biting the table edge. The head was balanced

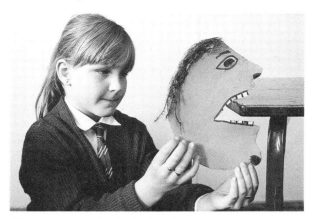

Figure 8 Sabrina's balancing mouth

on one of the teeth while the model was balanced by a bolt through the chin (figure 8).

Kassandra, Sabrina's friend, had drawn a copy of the balancing head. Her teacher accepted this but made a point of asking Kassandra how she would try to make her model a little different from her friend's. Encouraged by her teacher, Kassandra became confident enough to change her idea to include a body and to have the figure balancing comically on his chin.

Making the models

As the children finish their drawings, they will want to start making their models. It is useful to have the materials and tools they will need readily available, perhaps in labelled boxes. A word about not being wasteful would be appropriate here, since young children often have a peculiar tendency to cut the shapes they need from the centre of a large piece of card or fabric! The tools you put out for the children will probably include those that have been used before, such as scissors, but may include new ones, such as pliers and craft knives. A word about safety will be essential if this is the case.

Tools

Craft knives may be used to cut thick card or plastic and should be used with care. See page 93 for safety advice.

Pliers will present few safety problems to young children but it is worth showing them how to cut wire efficiently with them. As with cutting thick card with scissors, the closer the material is to the pivot of the tool the less effort

will be needed. Some pairs of pliers have side notches specifically designed for wire cutting. Children may find these easier to use. Inevitably there will be those in your group who are not strong enough to cut certain wires. They will have to enlist your help or that of a stronger friend.

There is a technique for shaping wire which you may find useful to describe to the children. It is better if the job can be done by hand as more control can be exercised, but if the length of wire is short this may not always be possible. A simple rule is to grip the end of a short piece of wire with the pliers and manipulate the wire by hand. If the wire is very short (say 5 cm), then two pairs of pliers may be required, one for gripping the end of the wire and the other for manipulating it.

In addition to the tools mentioned above, a paper hole punch may come in handy for making clean holes in paper, card or plastic. A heavy duty one will accommodate thick card and plastic. A pair of compasses will allow smaller holes to be worked in the material, perhaps to accommodate a piece of wire or thread.

Materials

Those using card will find it relatively easy to cut the shapes they need. A variety of collage material can be glued to the card, such as tissue, fabrics and wool to enhance the appearance of the model. Alternatively, the model could be painted and then varnished for an effective finish, or simply coloured using crayons or felt tip pens.

Plastic can usually be cut with scissors and fixed together with staples, or if the surface is roughened PVA adhesive may work. Other adhesives designed specifically for plastics can be used. The designs on the side of some containers can be cleaned off using medium grade glasspaper or wire wool. However, one drawback to using plastics is that the usual water-based paints cannot easily be applied.

Some models could be made entirely of wire. However, skill will be needed to bend the wire into shape with hands or pliers. If you have a small engineer's vice that can be clamped to the desk this will be a great help. The florists wire that has already been mentioned may be too weak to support the model shape but 1.6 mm welding wire will usually work. This can be bought either in straight lengths or by weight.

Mobiles and Balancing

1 Cut a piece of card like this.

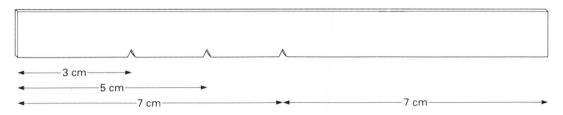

2 Try balancing your card with Plasticine in the ways shown below. Use all the Plasticine you have.

a

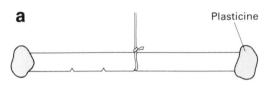

Plasticine

b

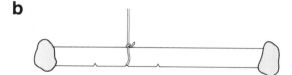

c

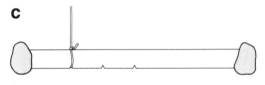

3 Now try changing this   into this:

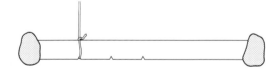

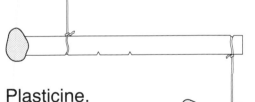

Always remember to use *all* your Plasticine.

4 Take two unequally sized blocks of wood and try to make your mobile balance.

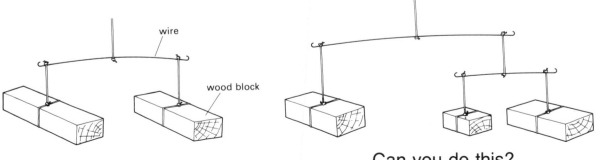

Can you do this?

Examples of balancing models

Some solutions for the teacher to have in mind are illustrated in figure 9

Figure 9 Some successful balancing models

Evaluating the finished product

An important part of the design process is finding time to evaluate the final model. This may take the form of a quiet talk with the maker. What are the successful features of the device? What improvements could be made (even if there is no time to make them)? The evaluation could take part within a small group of friends or it may be that the whole group is involved. The points to bring out are:

- Does the model do what it is supposed to do? Will it balance on the edge of a table? Will it stand upright? Does it do unusual things such as rock or wobble?
- Does the model look attractive. Is it well finished?
- Is the model strong enough to be used?

Children learn a lot from each other at this stage of the process. They have often been engrossed in their own project until now and will enjoy seeing how others have fared in fulfilling the same brief.

Similar projects

Make a mobile using card, plastic or wire shapes. The shapes can be suspended from wire rods or thin wooden ones. Choose shapes that form a theme such as fish, stars, insects, maths shapes or letters of the alphabet.

Initial research

Children will need to learn about balancing the arms of the mobile. The worksheet on page 17 might help them.

Some mobiles

The advice given in this chapter also applies to the shapes for the mobiles. Naturally, more work is involved because more shapes will be required. A minimum of two shapes is needed to make a mobile but four or five shapes will make the mobile more interesting, as shown in Figures 10 and 11.

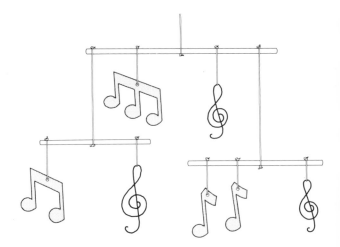

Figure 10 Wire and card mobile

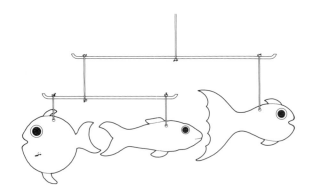

Figure 11 Hardboard fish mobile

Perhaps the most difficult part of this project is fixing the threads to the cross supports. It takes nimble hands to tie the threads and if the supports are lengths of wire the threads may slip. A spot of glue will secure the thread when you are sure it is in the correct position.

Centre of gravity

The centre of gravity of an object is the point where we imagine all the mass of the object to be concentrated. This point can be either inside or outside the object.

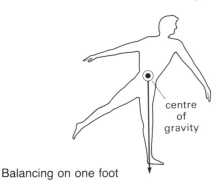

centre
of
gravity

Balancing on one foot

If our object is standing still, then its centre of gravity will have to be over the point or points of support. If the object is suspended and is stationary, its centre of gravity is below the point of support.

The centre of gravity of a person is located in the stomach area. If you want to stand on one foot, you have to keep your centre of gravity over that foot or you will fall. You manage this by moving your body slightly sideways and flexing the muscles in the foot on which you are standing or by waving your arms about frantically in order to maintain balance.

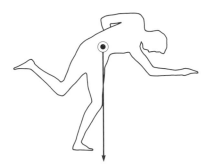

Falling

If, instead of hopping around, you decide to swing from the rafters, then your problems are greatly reduced. Your centre of gravity will now be below the point of support and you can't fall anywhere unless you let go!

Hanging

The models that the children are making need to have this form of stable equilibrium: the centre of gravity of each model must be *below* the point of support. This is generally achieved by arranging for the heavier parts of the model to be below the table surface or below the tightrope.

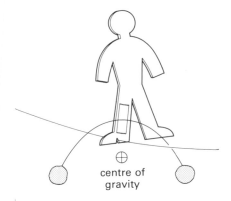

centre of
gravity

Centre of gravity *below* the tightrope

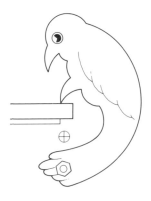

Centre of gravity *below* the table surface

2 Obstacle game

SUMMARY

The task
Design and make an obstacle course for a marble. The obstacles are to be made from small pieces of softwood which will then be glued to a hardboard base. The finished board will be tilted by hand so that the marble follows a marked line from one side of the board to the other.

Research
Difference between natural
and synthetic woods   20
Structure of natural woods   21
Marking wood to length   21
Cutting wood with a saw   22
Shaping and smoothing wood   23

Design
Design drawings   24

Making
Problems in construction: typical situations   24
Cutting wide sections of wood   26
Glueing   27
Finishing   27

Evaluation   27

Similar projects   27

Introducing the topic

The work in this chapter could well stem from a school topic on toys and games. All children will be familiar with games of one sort or another. Through discussion they will come to appreciate the need for clear rules to a game and the fact that the game should be suitably challenging. They will have come across small hand-held games containing ball bearings and will readily understand the idea of an obstacle race from their early sports days. We can combine these two ideas in the following task.

THE TASK
Design and make an obstacle course for a marble. The obstacles are to be made from small pieces of softwood which will then be glued to a hardboard base. The finished board will be tilted by hand so that the marble follows a marked path from one side of the board to the other.

The softwood required for this project can be purchased in small quantities from a woodyard. It is possible that some small off-cuts of wood have already been collected in school. The use of one or more woodworking benches with a vice attached would be useful, though not essential – a protected desk top with a removable vice will do. Some simple tools will be required to work the wood and these are described in the following pages. Furthermore, children will find it easier to manipulate this new material if they have taken a brief look at the structure of both natural and synthetic woods.

Natural and synthetic woods

It is important to show children the difference between natural and synthetic wood because this will affect the way in which these materials are handled. If possible, show them examples of softwoods and contrast these with the denser, often darker hardwoods. Then add examples of hardboard, chipboard, plywood and blockboard. Some of the synthetic woods may have a wood or plastic veneer on their surfaces so that they look like natural wood. If a piece of pine and a piece of hardboard are compared, the children should be able to point out the significant differences between them. The softwood will have a directional grain whilst the hardboard will be fibrous and without a directional grain. The children may guess that the hardboard has been manufactured whilst the softwood has been cut directly from a tree and then perhaps smoothed with a plane.

Structure of natural woods

Natural wood comes, of course, from a tree. We can think of a tree as being a bundle of tough fibres glued very strongly together. If we suppose that the piece of wood we have taken from the tree is like a bundle of straws held together tightly by elastic bands (figure 1), then we can give children an idea of what will happen if it is treated in the wrong way.

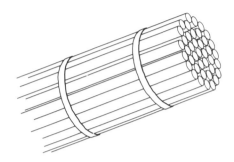

Figure 1 Straws model to show the fibrous structure of wood

The straws, or the fibres in the wood, make up the grain. It is the grain which makes the wood strong when you try to pull or squeeze it longways, or try to bend it. However, if we drive a nail into wood, then the 'glue' that holds these fibres will break (figure 2) and the

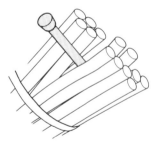

Figure 2 Demonstration of how wood splits

wood may split lengthwise. This weakness in the grain is especially noticeable when we try to shape the wood across the grain, as in figure 3.

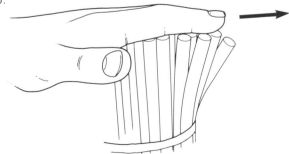

Figure 3 The effect of working across the grain

If we use a rasp or glasspaper on a piece of wood, it is best to try to move in the direction of the grain, as shown in figure 4, and not as shown in figure 5.

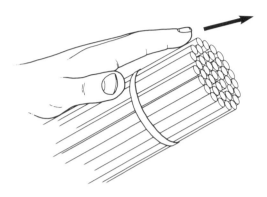

Figure 4 Working with the grain

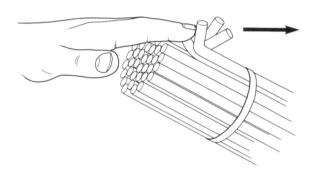

Figure 5 Working against the grain

Marking wood to length

The children will not need to use the special tool called a try-square for marking their wood in this exercise because the wood they cut will be of a narrow section. However, they will need to be reminded how to use a ruler correctly and to make a clear pencil mark on the wood (figure 6). Children are fond of sawing off pieces of wood by pure guesswork.

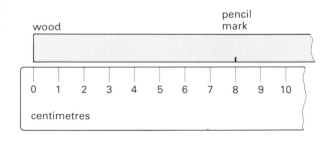

Figure 6 Marking wood to length

Cutting wood with a saw

A tenon saw is more efficient for cutting any but the smallest pieces of wood, but young children often find it too large to handle. So they can be given a choice of this or the smaller junior hacksaw illustrated in figure 7.

A bench hook (figure 7) is a useful way of holding the wood to be cut – with or without the help of a woodworking vice. Children sometimes forget to use this in their enthusiasm (or haste), but for safety's sake they must have a securely held piece of wood, so they may need to be reminded.

Figure 7 From left to right: tenon saw, junior hacksaw and bench hook

Cutting a piece of wood to length

SAW Secure the bench hook in a vice, if possible. If not, simply hook it over the bench or table (figure 8). Make sure the wood is properly marked to length using a pencil and ruler

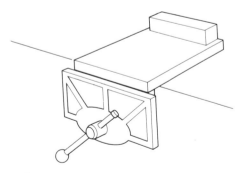

Figure 8 Securing a bench hook in a vice

(figure 9). Hold the wood against the bench hook block, as shown in figure 10, and start cutting at the end of the pencil line with the saw at an angle (figure 11).

Sawing carefully backwards and forwards, bring the saw down to a horizontal position to

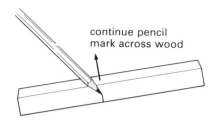

Figure 9 Marking the wood for sawing

continue pencil mark across wood

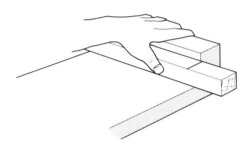

Figure 10 Holding the wood against the bench hook

Figure 11 Starting to saw along the pencil line

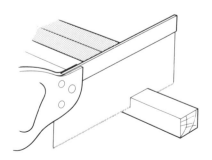

Figure 12 Bringing the saw down horizontally

make a groove across the wood (figure 12). Carry on cutting down until the piece is cut free (figure 13). Tell the children to keep the saw upright at all times and try not to twist it in the wood. If they get tired, tell them to take a rest – there's no hurry.

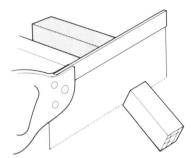

Figure 13 The finishing cut

There are other ways of holding wood so that it can be sawn securely. A lot depends on the size of the wood and the particular cut to be made. These methods, however, can be introduced to the children at a later date.

It would be wise at this point to allow the children to practise cutting some small-sectioned scraps of wood.

Shaping and smoothing wood

Wood can be shaped using a variety of tools. If the amount of wood to be removed is small, a file or rasp may be suitable. A selection of these is illustrated in figure 14.

Figure 14 Files and rasps, including the plane-like Surform

FILE, RASP, GLASSPAPER

The wood is best held in a vice and, of course, should first be marked to length with pencil. Care must be taken to work with the grain of the wood and never against it. It is often easier to move the file or rasp in a horizontal direction, so position the wood at an angle in the vice, as illustrated in figure 15. Generally the children should hold the tool with both hands, one on the handle and the other on the other end of the tool, and move smoothly in one direction only (not back and forth), as in

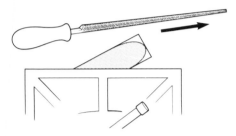

Figure 15 The correct position of the workpiece

Figure 16 Holding a Surform

figure 16. Get the children to turn the wood round in the vice, especially if they are trying to curve its end grain.

All shaped or cut pieces of wood should be smoothed with medium grade glasspaper (also called abrasive paper and sandpaper). If the children work hard with the glasspaper, they

Figure 17 Sanding block

can bring up the grain in the wood and make it look very attractive. It is best to get them to hold the glasspaper round a sanding block, as shown in figure 17. The glasspaper will be more effective if occasionally they clear the sanded particles from the block by patting it sharply with their free hand.

Design drawings

When the children understand the limitations of working with a resistant material such as wood, they will be ready to make some design drawings for their game. This is a good opportunity to give the children experience in drawing a full-scale plan-view of their model. If the baseboard of the game is a piece of hardboard or plywood, they should begin by drawing this on the paper. It could be a standard rectangular shape, or perhaps some will choose a rhombus or a triangle.

The next stage is to draw the route that the marble will take on its journey from one side of the board to the other. This can be done initially with pencil within the boundaries of the board shape. Encourage the children to create some interesting moves such as right-angled or hair-pin bends. Some marbles could 'loop the loop' and there should also be some hazards on the way.

Once the route has been settled, the children should put in the features, made of wood pieces, that will force the marble to take this path. Blind alleys, slight inclines and tunnels are a few of the obstacles that the children might use. Holes in the board would be a good

idea but the children will probably not have the expertise at this stage to make these, so it would be reasonable to avoid them. The children may ask to put nails or screws into their board, but this is not advisable with such a thin baseboard. If the children stick to obstacles that can be glued to the baseboard, they will have sufficient scope to explore a whole range of ideas.

The children should be aware of the wood sizes that are available, so ask them to make these widths apparent on their drawing. Encourage them to use a ruler to draw the straight edges of the wood pieces and get them to check at all times that the marble they have been given will fit between the obstacles they have drawn. It may be necessary to point out to some children that they can use large blocks of wood and posts on their board, as well as narrow sections. A variety of these are illustrated in figure 18.

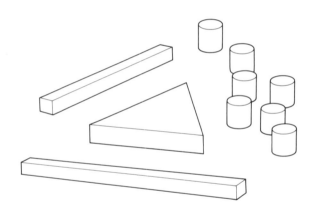

Figure 18 **Blocks and posts from which to make 'obstacles'**

If the children are adding any unusual features to their game, such as tunnels or rough surfaces, then they may wish to make separate drawings of these to show the detail.

When the drawings are finished, you may ask your children to mark in the true lengths of the pieces of wood on the diagram in readiness for the construction of the game.

Making the boardgame

It is impossible to predict all the problems that might arise in the construction of the boardgame but the following situations may serve to illustrate some of them.

Dannie's cutting problems

Dannie had found a piece of wood which was too wide for his purposes, but he intended to mark it out and saw it down the middle to make two equal narrow strips. His teacher luckily noticed this just before he started to saw the wood.

'I think we can save you some hard work, Dannie,' she said, as he lined up his wood awkwardly on the bench hook. 'How wide do you want your wood to be?'

After a moment of hesitation, Dannie replied that he wanted it about 1 cm wide.

'Then let's find a piece that is already that width so that you only have to cut it to length. That will mean about ten hours less sawing!' his teacher exaggerated.

Together they found a length of wood that was about 1 cm wide and Dannie's teacher pointed out how easy it was going to be to cut it across, rather than make the extremely awkward cut down the length of the other piece, as Dannie had originally planned.

As work progresses on the obstacle courses, the children will find they have a number of small problems to solve concerning the shaping of their pieces of wood. There are certain techniques to learn that make cutting and shaping wood safer and more efficient, but often commonsense is required to tackle individual problems.

Sarah's curved path

Sarah wanted her marble to follow a curved path at one point but didn't know how she was going to curve her piece of wood (figure 19.) Sarah's teacher knew, by experience, of a number of ways of shaping the curve. A coping saw could be used to cut out the piece of unwanted wood or a chisel could be employed to do the same job. Sarah, however, was only able to use a rounded rasp or a Surform so she

would have to be shown a way of using one of these tools to achieve her desired effect.

Sarah's teacher demonstrated how to secure the wood in a vice and how to hold a rasp. He pointed out that moving the rasp directly across the grain might cause parts of the wood to split away, so he showed Sarah how to move diagonally along the length of wood using a curving movement (figure 20).

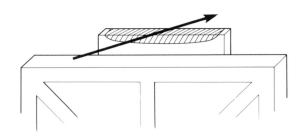

Figure 20 Using a rasp to shape the curve Sarah wanted

Lisa's round-edged walls

Lisa wanted to round off the tops of all her 'walls of wood' so she was shown how to use the small Surform. Again, a vice was necessary. Lisa was asked to feel the bottom of the Surform so that she could tell in which direction to push it so that it would actually cut. There had been instances in the past where children had been working hard to no avail by pushing the Surform backwards.

Lisa was encouraged to finish her pieces of shaped wood with medium glasspaper.

Jason and Savash's ridged pathway

Jason and Savash had a strange request. They wanted a ridged length of wood so that the marble would have a difficult run (figure 21).

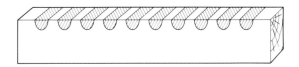

Figure 21 Jason and Savash's idea

'We want to make a part of our game really difficult,' explained Jason, as he went into a detailed description of tunnels, alleyways and 'railings'.

Figure 19 Sarah's problem

Obstacle game

Their teacher suggested that the boys use the small round file across the grain of their wood to achieve the desired effect (figure 22). Because it was a fine file they wouldn't have too much trouble with torn fibres of wood.

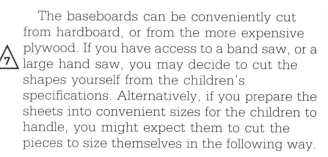

Figure 22 Using a file to achieve the right effect Jason and Savash wanted

Putting it together

As the children cut, shape and smooth their obstacles they should be asked to place the finished pieces on their diagram to ensure that they fit. Every now and then the marble could be run between the wooden blocks to make sure that the finished game will run smoothly.

Figure 23 Fixing the 'obstacles'

The baseboards can be conveniently cut from hardboard, or from the more expensive plywood. If you have access to a band saw, or a large hand saw, you may decide to cut the shapes yourself from the children's specifications. Alternatively, if you prepare the sheets into convenient sizes for the children to handle, you might expect them to cut the pieces to size themselves in the following way.

Cutting wide sections of wood

Some pieces of wood are too wide and also too thin to be cut effectively on the bench hook. Sheets of hardboard or plywood are good examples of this. The following method is one that children can use to cut these.

1 Measure up and mark the wood with a pencil and ruler (figure 24).

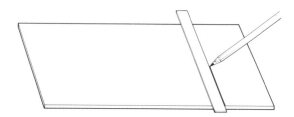

Figure 24 Measuring the sheet and marking it

2 Cramp the wood so that the saw line overhangs the edge of the bench (figure 25). A small piece of scrap wood should be used to protect the piece to be sawn from the metal cramp.

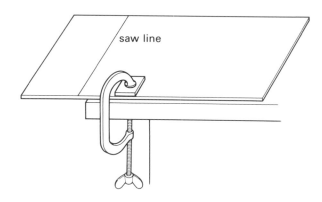

Figure 25 Sheet held in a cramp

3 Use a tenon saw (or a small hand saw) and begin cutting at the far edge of the wood (figure 26). It may be possible to use two hands on the saw handle and this will steady the saw cut.

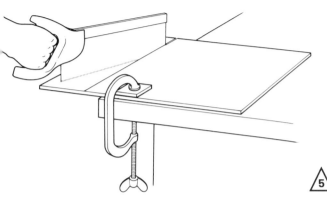

Figure 26 Cutting with a tenon saw

4 Blow away the sawdust so that the line can be followed carefully. The saw is kept at the same angle throughout the cut so a junior hacksaw will not work. As the end of the cut is approached, the child should ask a partner to support the piece being cut off and saw more gently so as not to split the last piece of wood.

When wood is cut on a bench hook, the fibres at the base of the wood are supported until they are cut by the saw. A fairly clean cut is therefore obtained. When the fibres are not supported, as in the case described above, they may fray and leave an untidy jagged edge which has to be sanded smooth.

Glueing

When the baseboard has been cut to shape, get the children to smooth the edges with glasspaper. The wood block obstacles can then be laid on the board in the correct positions. If it is clear that the marble will roll freely around the course, the shapes can be drawn round lightly with pencil to mark their positions and then removed. Glue the obstacles to the baseboard one at a time with PVA adhesive. Excess adhesive can be carefully wiped clear with a damp paper towel. The children must now allow time for the glue to set before trying their game.

Finishing

The course the marble should take must now be marked on the hardboard, perhaps with a thick felt pen or a carefully guided paintbrush. Encourage the children to try their game before putting the final touches to their work. They will need to be sure that the marble rolls freely and that the game is suitably challenging. There will still be time to make minor alterations if necessary.

Generally, it is possible to paint over softwoods with normal water-based paints, as long as they are mixed thickly. However, too much untidy paintwork at this stage might spoil the appearance of the game. You might like to encourage the children to leave the wood in its natural attractive state. A coat or two of polyurethane varnish could profitably be applied to the board whether it is painted or not. Clean the brushes thoroughly in white spirit and then hot soapy water.

Evaluating the finished product

You will probably find that the children will automatically evaluate their work as they proceed. It is usually valuable, however, to save some time at the end for the whole group to look at each other's work and make constructive comments. If your children can manage it they could be asked to mark each game out of ten for difficulty and perhaps a mark for its attractive qualities.

Similar projects

Design and make a table-top skittles game. The skittles will be cut and shaped from small-sectioned softwood and must be no taller than 10 centimetres. The skittles will be knocked over by a marble and the whole game must be small enough to play on a coffee table.

You may consider these additional features for your game: a launch ramp for the marble, and a simple barrier to prevent the marble rolling off the table.

Preliminary research

The children will need to appreciate the need to make clear-cut rules for the game and they

Obstacle game

will have to make the game sufficiently challenging to be interesting. Encourage them to discover these ideas themselves by taking part in the following exercise.

Give the children a wide variety of bits and pieces, such as card tubes, boxes, cotton reels, blocks of wood, marbles and tennis balls. Challenge them to invent a skittles game in a given period of time (say 40 minutes) by trying different arrangements of the materials available. Nothing is to be glued or fixed in any way. They should write a brief description of the rules for their game and be prepared to read these out and demonstrate the game to the group.

Making the table-top skittles game

The children will have to decide:

How many skittles to have.
How these will be placed on the table.
How to shape the skittles.
How to launch the marble.
How many rolls of the marble each player gets.
How to score.

Examples of skittle design

Figure 27 depicts the types of design that the children might come up with.

Figure 27 Some ideas for skittles

Hint: A problem may arise if the small skittles do not stand upright on the table because of a sloping saw cut. This can be easily overcome by glueing card bases to the skittles while the skittle is held upright. An excess of glue will compensate for the sloping base (figure 28).

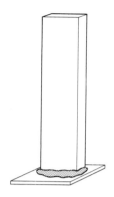

Figure 28 Putting a card base on a wonky skittle

3 Paddle boats

SUMMARY

The task

Design and make a toy paddle boat that moves as smoothly through the water as possible. The boat should be propelled by a paddle which is driven by the energy in a twisted elastic band. If there is time you may add features to the simple, solid hull to make it look more realistic.

Research

Design

Making

Evaluation

Similar projects   38

A model vehicle of any kind which can move holds a fascination for children, especially if they are involved in making the model themselves. Models that possess wheels or wings have special, technical problems that will need to be overcome. However, boats move easily on water, whether it be in a bowl, large sink or a pond. Almost any boat will be a success in some way or other, so this project is ideal for children with only a little experience in designing and making. While paddle boats can be made from any material that has strength and will float, softwood is the best material to use since it allows children to learn important skills in manipulating resistant materials whilst at the same time providing a versatile medium for a wide variety of designs. It is important, however, for children to realise that other materials, besides wood, can successfully be used in the construction of models, so it is worth discussing the use of metals and plastics for additional features on the boat. In this project it will be necessary to provide a more comprehensive set of tools and facilities.

Figure 1 Observing the action of a paddle

Besides a try-square and coping saw, a woodworkers' bench vice will now be essential.

This project will probably complement many themes that are already being explored in other lessons. It will fit in well with a topic on transport, or one on movement. Alternatively, a science topic, such as energy or water, might be a good starting point. Work on reference skills could be put to good use in the research that will be necessary for the boat design. If you are currently studying plans and maps, then the children will find this particularly useful when making their design drawings.

Getting started

If you want this truly to be a problem-solving exercise, then it is important not to show the children exactly how a boat might be made. At the same time, however, they need to be shown the principle by which the boat will be propelled. When this has been demonstrated, they should then be able to work out the hull design themselves. Perhaps it would be a good idea to start with a cardboard mock-up, which is obviously doomed to failure and ask them to improve upon it. Something like the model illustrated in figure 2 would do.

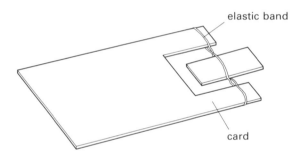

Figure 2 Card paddle boat ready to be improved

Show the children how the card paddle can be wound up and released. If you try it in a bowl of water they will soon see how hopeless it is and be ready to suggest improvements.

THE TASK
Design and make a toy paddle boat that moves as smoothly through the water as possible. The boat should be propelled by a paddle which is driven by the energy in a twisted elastic band. If there is time you may add features to the simple, solid hull to make it look more realistic.

The following points will need to be considered:

● Which materials would be better than card for making the hull, and why?
  Plastic – Does all plastic float? Do we have the tools and skills to make a hull shape?
  Wood – This would seem to be the ideal

material since it has strength and we know how to shape it. We also know that it floats.

● What shape could the hull be?

● Which materials would be best for the paddle? Plastic, polystyrene, plywood, hardboard?

● Where should the paddle be positioned? At the back, the middle or the front?

● What shape should the paddle be and how many blades could it have?

● How many elastic bands should be used and what size should they be?

● How will the elastic band be secured?

These discussion points are important in showing the children that the shape of the card model you have just made is not the only design possible for the boat. In fact, the permutations are endless, and the children will enjoy it all the more if you give them a sense of exploring uncharted territory.

Research

There are a number of profitable research exercises that the children could work through. A science investigation into the properties of a twisted elastic band would be one. However, perhaps more useful at this stage would be the use of reference books to find out about different hull designs. The children could be asked to make sketches of the different types of boat hull they have found, paying special attention to the overall plan view and the side view. Detailed drawings are unnecessary, just simple outline plans and side views will be sufficient. Given access to the appropriate books, they should be able to find examples of catamarans and trimarans, as well as the more conventional mono-hull vessels. If large sketches are made then these can be shown to the rest of the group with a reference to the book (and page number) from which the design was taken.

More research will be required later for the design of the paddle, but it is better to concentrate at first on designing and making the hull.

Shaping the hull

Before the children can be expected to draw their hull designs they will need to understand the limitations of the tools and materials they will be working with. They will probably also need to learn how to use some new tools.

Assuming the hulls will be solid and fashioned out of softwood, the children will need to cut their wood to length. This is a good opportunity to introduce the use of the try-square for marking out wood.

Marking out wood with a try-square

The try-square allows a line to be drawn across a piece of wood at right-angles to its length. This line can then be extended down the sides to act as a guideline when sawing vertically downwards (see figures 3 and 4), using the technique already described on page 22.

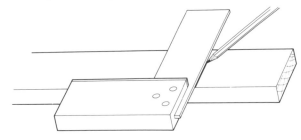

Figure 3 Marking the top of the wood with a try-square

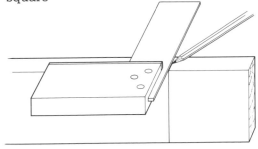

Figure 4 Marking the side of the wood with a try-square

You can give the children an interesting exercise at this point by asking them to accurately cut a short section of wood. Tell them you want a 15 cm length of wood that stands vertically on the bench. To achieve this it is essential that the wood is cut absolutely square. A try-square must be used and the wood has to be sawn very carefully. The test, when the children have finished, is to stand the blocks on the bench and see if any tilt. If a block does not stand at all, then it is probably a good idea to ask the child to try again, cutting the piece of wood to a length of 12 cm this time to avoid wasting wood. The squareness of the end of the wood can be tested accurately by using the try-square again, as shown in figure 5.

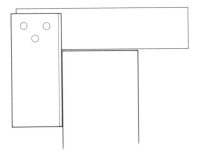

Figure 5 Testing the squareness of the end of a piece of wood using a try-square

After the children have cut their pieces of wood to length, they will then have to think about cutting the actual hull shape. This will almost certainly be symmetrical about a centre line and will probably involve cutting a curve using a coping saw. The symmetrical plan of the hull can best be achieved by folding some card in half and drawing half the hull on one side, about the fold. When this shape has been cut out, the card can be opened up and used as a template to transfer the hull shape to the wooden block (figures 6). Before the children make their design decisions, show them how the hull could be shaped using a coping saw.

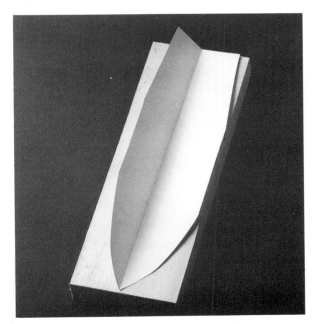

Figure 6 Transferring the shape of a symmetrical hull to a block of wood

COPING SAW

Cutting curves with a coping saw

Let the children place the wood in a vice, with the line that is to be cut as near to the vertical as possible. The wood should be fairly low in the vice to avoid excess vibration (figure 7). Using two hands to hold the coping saw handle, show the children how to saw downwards, carefully trying to follow the marked line. The wood may have to be turned gradually in the vice to achieve this.

Figure 7 Cutting wood with a coping saw

Each curve is different so there are no hard and fast rules for cutting curves. It is essential, however, that the saw blade is kept at right-angles to the wood surface. Children will find this difficult at first and may break some of the thin blades, so have some spares available! If a blade breaks it is not dangerous and children

COPING SAW

can quickly learn to replace it, as shown in figure 8.

A useful feature of the coping saw blade is that it can be turned through an angle relative to the frame. This can be an advantage when cutting awkward curves in larger pieces of wood but should not be necessary when cutting the hull shapes. If the blade is turned like this, care should be taken to align the two blade supports at each end of the frame so that the blade is never twisted.

Cutting curves with an Abrafile

Abrafiles are similar to coping saws in that they can cut curves in wood. Instead of a saw blade, however, they have a fine file stretched across a frame. This means that the sawing motion can take place in any direction. Children may find an Abrafile easier to use because it does not have to be oriented, but it does not saw as efficiently as a blade so the job will take more effort and time. Abrafiles are best used when the thickness of the wood is not too great, as in hardboard or thin plywood.

Choosing the dimensions of the hull

The final piece of information that the children will need to consider before they draw their design for the hull on paper, is the dimensions of the wood available. You will probably provide a selection of wood of different widths and thicknesses from which the children will cut their hulls. It would be pointless for a child to design a hull which has a maximum width of 8 cm when the widths of the wood available are 5, 10 and 12 cm. In a large, well-equipped workshop wood can be sawn or planed down to the exact size required. However, it is unlikely you will have these facilities so it is best to

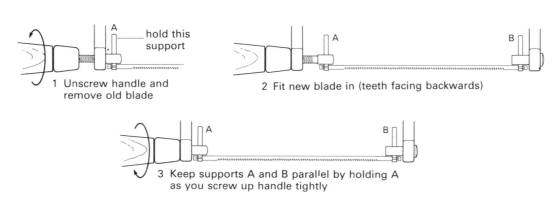

Figure 8 Replacing a broken coping saw blade

choose projects which are flexible and which suit the conditions to hand. With these constraints in mind, show the children the dimensions of the wood available before they begin their design drawings and ask them to adapt their measurements to suit those available.

Design drawings

The children will probably have been introduced to the idea of plan and side view of a boat hull when they did their research. If not it is certainly a good time to give children practice in using this method of design drawing now. They will probably find it easier if you give them squared paper to work on. Encourage them to draw the plan and the side elevation on the same sheet of paper, one directly under the other, so that the two views can be easily compared. Figure 9 illustrates how this should be done. Notice how features on the plan are directly above the same features on the side view, and how the vertical lines on the paper act as guides to where these features should be.

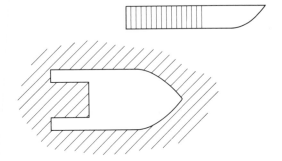

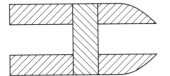

Figure 10 **Some different types of shading**

illustrates different types of shading that can be used to good effect. Figure 11 illustrates the type of design drawing you could expect to get from children after you have discussed the relevant aspects of the design with them.

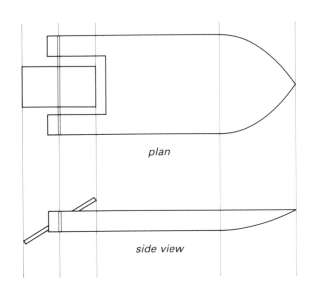

Figure 9 **Design drawing showing plan and side views**

A full-sized drawing would be appropriate here if you can supply the children with a big enough piece of paper. Alternatively, they could use a 1:2 scale. Try and encourage the children to add neat, clear labelling. Suggest that they shade their drawings with a pencil crayon to make it stand out. Figure 10

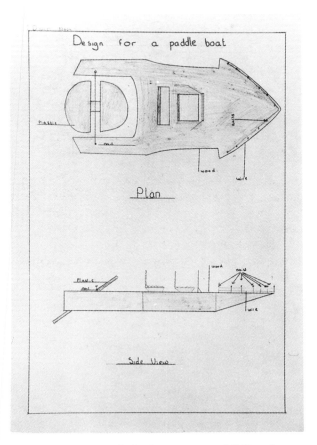

Figure 11 **Typical design proposal following a searching discussion**

Making the hull

As the drawings are completed and checked the children will be ready to begin making the hull. They will need to select wood that is of the correct width and thickness. It is probably worth reiterating the importance of cutting wood so that there is minimum wastage (figure 12).

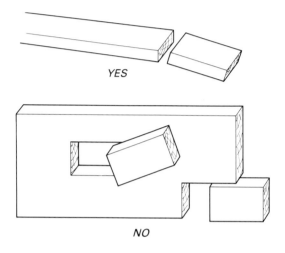

Figure 12 Cutting wood efficiently

With the thorough preparation that has just been described, this phase should run fairly smoothly. The following situations, however, illustrate some of the issues that may arise.

Mary's catamaran hull

Mary had chosen a catamaran hull consisting of two narrow, pointed pieces of wood joined by a single cross-member (figure 13). The cross member was joined to each hull by a simple butt joint. Mary's teacher, however, was concerned about the strength of this design

and decided to discuss the issue with Mary before she had gone too far with the construction. Conscious of good problem-solving techniques, they both explored as many possible improvements as they could.

'I could glue more strips of wood across the hulls.'

'OK, but would you then have room for the paddle?'

'Could I nail a platform of plywood across the hulls like this?' Mary drew a small sketch on a scrap of paper.

'Yes that's a good idea. Now what else would do it?'

Mary and her teacher went on to discuss using dowel rods which could be fitted into holes in the hull, setting the cross member into the top of the hulls, and using reinforcing triangles of wood at the butt joints. Figure 14 illustrates some solutions to the problem that they came up with.

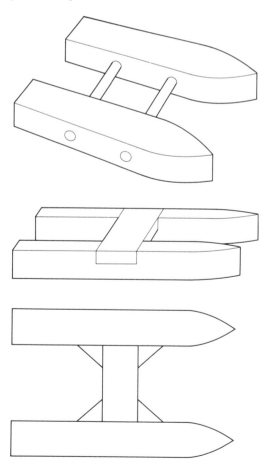

Figure 14 Ideas for strengthening a catamaran hull

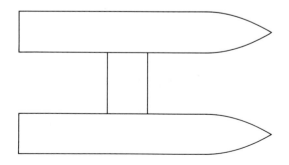

Figure 13 Mary's catamaran hull

Jason's hull shape

Jason wanted to cut a section out of the end of his hull to take the paddle. He had decided how big this needed to be and had drawn in the shape to be cut out. Now he wanted to know how he could cut this piece out (figure 15).

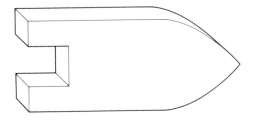

Figure 15 Jason's hull shape

His teacher advised him to use a combination of two saws, a tenon saw for cutting the vertical straight lines, then a coping saw to cut across the hull. The hull was put in a vice to help this operation. However, care had to be taken when the coping saw met the bottom of the tenon saw cut. The saw had to be drawn rapidly back and forth on the spot while it was turned at right-angles.

Julie's central paddle

Julie had decided to experiment by positioning the paddle right in the middle of the hull. After having drawn on the wooden hull the shape to be cut from it, she was then concerned about how she was going to do it. Her teacher advised her to drill a 6 mm ($\frac{1}{4}$ inch) hole inside the shape. As Julie had not yet learned how to use a hand drill her teacher did this part for her. However, after this initial help, Julie was then able to continue with the rest of the operation. Her teacher described how to proceed from there:

'Loosen the blade from a coping saw and thread it through the hole we have drilled. Then tension the blade back on to the frame.' (See figure 16.)

'Now position the wood in the vice so that you are about to saw downwards along one of the lines you have drawn.'

Julie's teacher watched her do this and then showed her how to cut round the right-angled corner with rapid saw movements, practically on the spot.

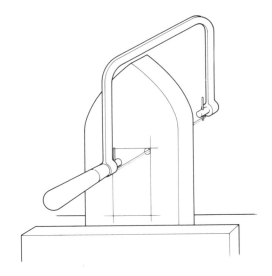

Figure 16 Preparing to cut the central hole

When the piece was finally removed, the coping saw had to be dismantled again to remove it from the hull. Julie was then encouraged to smooth the sides carefully with a rasp, trying to move with the grain as much as possible.

Many children will decide to smooth and shape the front of their hulls and this can best

Figure 17 Shaping the front section of the hull

35

be achieved by using a Surform or a rasp with the hull held firmly in a vice. The planing action should take place in the direction of the grain of the woods as described on page 23. Once this has been done the hull should be smoothed with medium grade glasspaper.

Designing and attaching the paddle

When a number of children are ready to fix paddles to their boats, it will be worth gathering them round to discuss the issue.

Sort out the variations in paddle shape that could be used. Rectangles are fine but can always be improved upon. You should explore the possibility of using materials other than wood – plastic spoons, flat lollipop sticks, thin sheets of aluminium (these can be cut with an old pair of scissors). Polystyrene from meat trays can be easily shaped and cork hubs with blades can also be used to good effect.

Using a card model, show the children how multiple blades can be made (figure 18). They will have to work harder to produce a wooden one but, if they want to have a go, hardboard would probably be the best material to use.

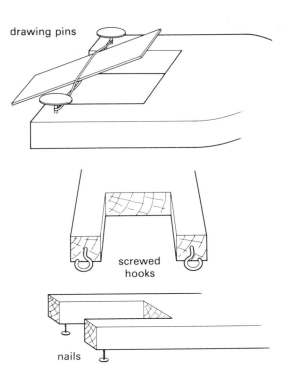

Figure 19 Three ways to attach the elastic band

of positions. Figure 19 illustrates some of these. Figure 20 shows some paddle designs for you to have in mind in case the children get stuck.

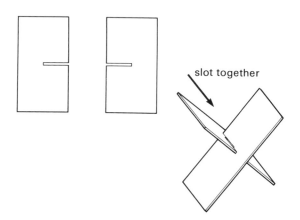

Figure 18 Making a four-bladed paddle

Figure 20 Some paddles designed and made by nine-year-olds

There are various ways in which the blade can be fixed to the elastic so that it does not float away at the end of its run. Tie a knot in the elastic each side of the paddle, use drawing pins or staples or in some cases leave the paddle free.

The ends of the elastic band can be attached to the hull in a variety of ways and in a variety

Improving the paddle design

Children who have not completely understood the function of a paddle will often begin by making a simple one that is much too small. When they try this on their boat's maiden voyage, they will be disappointed to find that practically nothing happens, apart from a quick splash. However, the useful thing about leaving children to design their own paddles is that mistakes can quite quickly be rectified and valuable lessons can be learnt. A lot of useful work can be done in the analysis of a poorly performing boat.

- Does the paddle catch or rub on the side of the boat?
- Is the paddle pushing enough, i.e. is it large enough?
- Could the paddle be curved to hold more water? Should it be made of plastic to achieve this?
- Does the elastic release its energy too quickly, and why?
- Does the elastic band get caught between the hull and paddle when it is wound up?
- Could the elastic band be fixed in a better position?
- Is the elastic band too strong/not strong enough?
- Does the boat take a curved path rather than a straight one and what can be done about it?

The following illustrates a problem that children often encounter.

Melanie was complaining that she couldn't twist her paddle up very far because the band got caught between the paddle and the sides of the boat.

'It needs more space to wind up,' said Lisa, who had been thinking about her problem for some time now.

'She'll have to make another hull,' said Stephen pessimistically.

'No, she can bring her elastic band on to the top like mine,' said Abdul as he showed Melanie the hooks on top of his hull.

'Could Melanie do anything to her paddle?' prompted her teacher, who wanted to explore as many ideas as possible.

'But if I make it narrower,' protested Melanie, 'then it will have less push.'

'You could make it smaller in the middle where the elastic winds up,' offered Lisa, 'but keep it wider at the ends where it pushes.'

And so the discussion continued around a number of solutions to Melanie's problem.

Eventually she took up Lisa's suggestion and redesigned the paddle shape to leave more room for the twisted elastic band.

Adding the finishing touches

When the children have perfected their motor system, they might like to add features to the deck of their hull, such as a bridge or cabins. Some might like to use nails and fine wire to make a rail around the perimeter, or perhaps a mast could be made from stronger wire. An imaginative windscreen made from a piece of clear plastic from a lemonade bottle, might also be suggested by someone.

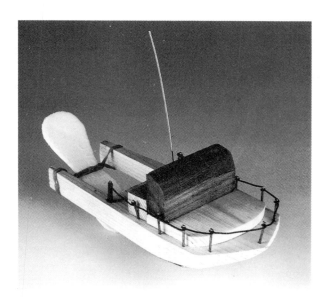

Figure 21 Designed and made by an 11-year-old

If the boats are wet because of extensive trials, they should be allowed to dry out before any parts of them are painted and varnished. It would, of course, be unwise to use water-based paints or felt pens without protecting these with a coat of polyurethane varnish, especially if the boat is going to be used on water in the future. Naturally, a paint and varnish finish will only look its best on well-sanded wood.

Evaluating the finished boat

The process of evaluation – analysis and improvements – will have been occurring ever since the first paddle was wound up. If the

Paddle boats

children have been designing their boats for speed, then time trials or a lighthearted race over a large expanse of water will be necessary. Some boats may have been made with duration in mind. If you have a pond or large trough allow the boats to run back and forth, turning them immediately they reach the water's edge. Part of the final evaluation may be on the appearance of the vessel, though this will be of relatively minor importance compared with performance. Rather than criticise the poor features of each boat, ask the group to point out what they consider are the successes of both their own and their friends' models.

Similar projects

Wooden-hulled boats can be driven using other arrangements than those already described in this chapter. The sketches shown in figures 22 illustrates three alternatives.

Elastic-band driven axle

In this model the paddles are first wound backwards to create tension in the elastic band and then released when the boat is in the water. It is important that the axle runs smoothly in its supports. It can be made from wooden dowel or straight lengths of welding wire. The paddles can be slotted into hubs of cork or broom handle.

Propeller-driven boat

More advice on propellers can be found in Chapter 5.

Sail boat

There are many other variations of the sail configuration than the one shown in this model. If the boat is driven by a sail, it is likely to need a weighted keel or centre board. In the classroom it could be driven by a fan or hairdryer across a sink or paddling pool. Outside a fair breeze will be needed.

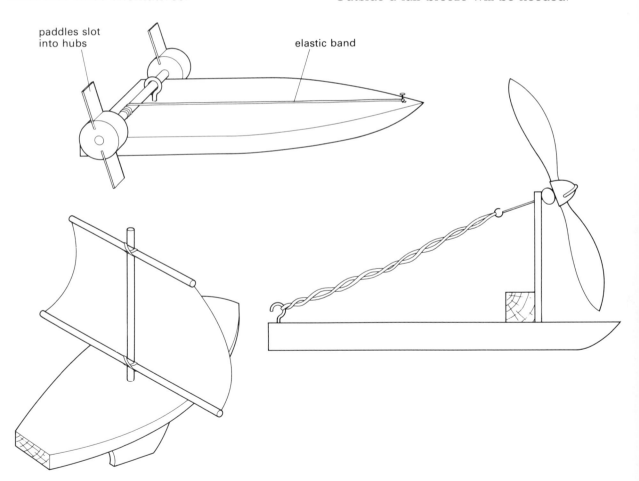

paddles slot into hubs

elastic band

Figure 22 Other methods of propulsion

ABOUT . . .

Streamlined shapes

As the children think about the best shape for their hull, you may want to introduce the idea of the ideal streamlined shape. This is the shape which would offer the least resistance to forward movement in a particular medium, such as water. Shaping for a streamlined effect is found in aircraft design, fast cars and some animals. A submarine shaped like a fish has a streamlined shape. An aircraft wing, besides providing lift, must also offer as little resistance to forward motion as possible.

There are a number of well-known scientific investigations into the best streamlined shape in water and these would provide an excellent research exercise for the paddle boat design, if there is time. One involves a long trough filled with water, various hull shapes from balsa or other softwood and a thread and pulley system for pulling these along the trough. Those taking the shortest time to travel the length of the trough have the best streamlined hulls. Alternatively, fill a glass or Perspex tube with water and allow different Plasticine shapes to fall while being timed. As long as the falling body stays clear of the side of the tube, you should find that the standard streamline shape as illustrated below works best. As this shape moves forward, the fluid in which it is travelling is able to flow smoothly in layers over its surface. The tendency of the fluid to mix and swirl behind the shape is called turbulence and creates a force called drag, which hinders movement. Streamlined shapes are therefore designed to minimise drag.

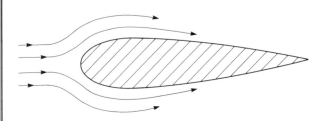

An ideal streamlined shape

Energy changes

Energy, and the way one kind changes into another, is a fundamental concept in science. The design of the paddle boat gives us a good opportunity to talk casually in terms of energy thus enabling the children involved to develop their understanding. We can talk in terms of the energy stored in the twisted elastic band. More twists and more elastic bands would mean more energy is stored.

Energy will be wasted if it isn't all used to push the boat forward.

When we wind the paddle up, we transform energy stored in our muscles into that stored in the elastic. When the boat is set in the water and released, the stored elastic energy is transformed into the movement energy of the boat and, incidentally, the water. Some energy is, of course, transformed into small amounts of heat, as friction occurs in various parts of the paddle mechanism. The movement energy of the boat and the water is also converted through friction to heat energy, the amount of which is too small for us to notice.

Action and reaction

So how does the boat move forward? The answer is by pushing the water backwards. Isaac Newton stated this simple principle thus: for every action there is an equal and opposite reaction. So, for example, if you are standing on a perfectly slippery floor and want to move forward, one thing you can do is to throw something hard in the other direction. The paddle boat, and any other motor boat for that matter, is designed to do just this. If the paddle boat is held still in the water the children can see the water being pushed away by the paddle. The more water that is pushed the better the boat will run. Hence the need to design the most efficient paddle.

4 Wheels and levers

SUMMARY

The task
Design and make a toy that has a part that moves up and down through the action of an eccentric wheel operated by turning a handle. The toy must look attractive and be fun to play with.

Research

Design

Making

Evaluation   49

Similar projects   50

About . . .

In this project children can learn about the scientific principles of the lever and the eccentric wheel, or cam, and about some of their technological applications. This is another idea, similar to the marble game in Chapter 2, that could develop from a school topic on toys. The principles involved are also closely associated with the workings of certain machines, so a visit to a science museum or a suitable manufacturer might provide an alternative starting point.

The children will need to use skills they have already learnt, such as the ability to saw sections of wood and shape them with the appropriate tools. In addition to this, they will be introduced to the new skill of making holes in wood with a hand drill.

THE TASK
Design and make a toy that has a part that moves up and down through the action of an eccentric wheel operated by turning a handle. The toy must look attractive and be fun to play with.

Investigating the effect of an eccentric wheel

The children will need to understand how an eccentric wheel can produce a lateral movement, so it might be helpful to begin with a simple demonstration.

Pin a card wheel to a wooden dowel axle so that it is off-centre, as shown in figure 1. As the wheel is turned round, the children will see that it 'wobbles'. Explain that engineers often want to change a turning movement in a machine into an up-and-down or side-to-side movement, as they have just seen. Examples of

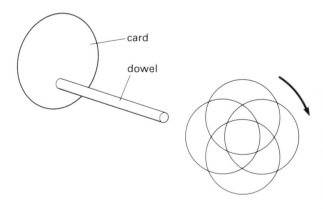

Figure 1 Demonstrating the eccentric wheel

this type of action can be found in sewing machines, some pull-along toys, or a forge hammer worked by a turning water wheel.

You might find the worksheets on pages 41 and 42 useful in helping the children to understand these ideas better.

Worksheet

Wheels and Levers 1

Draw a circle of radius 2 cm on a
piece of corrugated cardboard.
Cut it out.

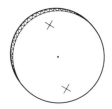

Use a compass point to make a hole at the points marked X in the
picture. These holes should be big enough for paper fasteners to fit
through.

Take a piece of stiff card and make
a hole in the same way in the
middle of it.

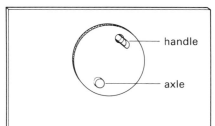

Fix the cardboard wheel to the card
base as shown. One paper
fastener is the handle, the other
is the off-centre axle of the
wheel.

Turn your wheel and see what happens.
Draw round your wheel in
lots of different positions.

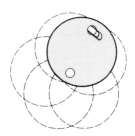

Make a card lever like this and fix it to the card base with a paper
fastener in the position shown.

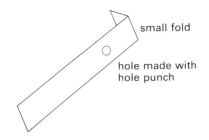

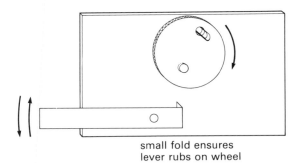

small fold ensures
lever rubs on wheel

Turn the wheel so that the lever moves up and down.

Try using levers which have their holes in different positions. What
happens?

What happens if you use bigger wheels?

Wheels and Levers 2

Try and make these models just by looking at the pictures.

1

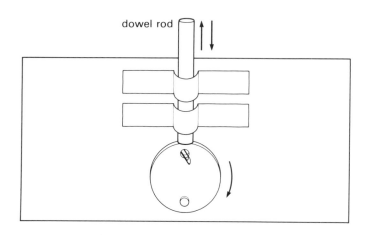

dowel rod

2

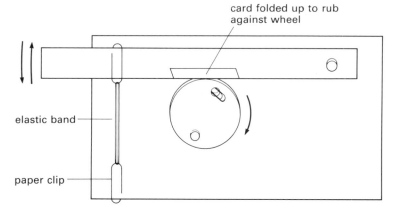

card folded up to rub against wheel

elastic band

paper clip

3

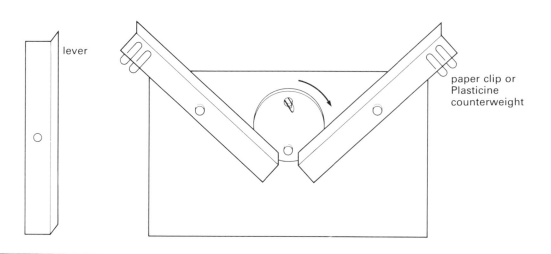

lever

paper clip or Plasticine counterweight

Design ideas

In keeping with the design principle that a number of solutions should always be considered before settling on a particular one, ask the children to suggest a range of ideas that would be suitable for a wheel-and-lever toy. These are some of the suggestions that they might come up with:

Head popping up over a wall

See-saw

Crocodile opening and closing its mouth

Elephant waving its trunk

Ship at sea

Person waving arm(s)

Coffin slowly opening

As the children already have some of the skills needed to cut and shape wood, it would be sensible to ask them to use this material to make their toy. However, it might be a useful exercise at this stage to discuss the range of other materials available, e.g. plastic or metal, that they could use.

Design drawings

Ask the children to decide on one idea and draw it. Encourage them to draw their idea full size, if possible, and include the following:

- A view of the front showing the general idea, the colour scheme, and relative sizes of the component parts.

- A view of the back showing the size of the wheel, the position of the wheel and moving parts, the pivot points – dowel rod, nail or screw.

Extra planning

The positioning of the wheel and lever will be critical in the finished model, so it is strongly recommended that the children make a full-sized card model as part of their preparations. This can be altered at will until it works reasonably well. Measurements and positions can then be transferred directly to the wood.

Making the basic model

The main body of the toy can be cut from softwood 1 cm thick, or more. The wooden wheel should be attached to this by means of a dowel axle so that it rotates smoothly about an off-centre point. The dowel will need to be fitted into holes cut into the wheel and the body of the toy. As the wheel will have to be turned to make the toy work, a handle will have to be fitted to it (figure 3).

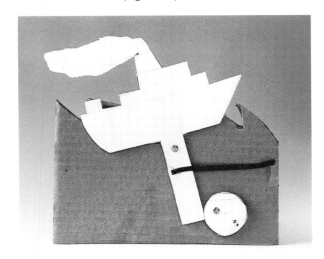

Figure 2 Card and corrugated paper mock-up

Inexpensive wooden wheels can be obtained from a number of suppliers these days. The wheels are cut from thin plywood and often have a central hole which, for the purpose of this exercise, can be ignored. A range of sizes should include diameters from 2 to 8 cm. This is by far the easiest way of supplying the children with wheels for their models. It is, however, possible for children to cut their own wheels from a broom handle or by cutting a circle from thin wood with a coping saw.

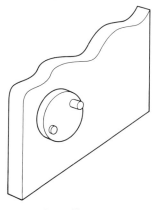

Figure 3 Fitting a handle to an eccentric wheel

Wheels and levers

If you want to supply your own wheels then you could cut these using an electric hand-held or pedestal drill with a hole cutting attachment, called a hole-saw (figure 4). The wheels can be cut from any scrap wood up to about 1 cm thick. This must be cramped securely to the bench, with a piece of scrap wood underneath to protect the bench. Hole-saws are too dangerous for children to use.

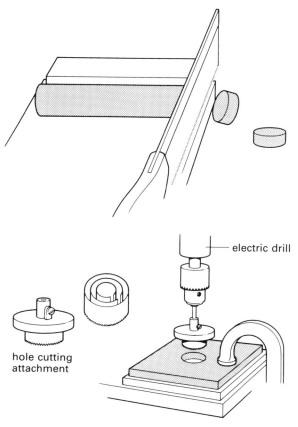

electric drill

hole cutting
attachment

Figure 4 Two ways of cutting wheels

Drilling holes

Children can drill holes in wood or plastic by using a hand drill and a drill bit of the appropriate size. They will require holes in the wheels and levers they are using in their models.

There are various types of hand drill or twist drill on the market at present. Children often find them quite hard to hold steady, so give them some practice and be prepared to have some of the smaller drill bits broken. The pistol grip drill would seem the obvious choice for youngsters to handle but this is the more expensive of the drills available (figure 5).

Figure 5 Hand drills and drill bits

The position in which a hole is to be drilled should be marked with a small cross or dot. (Children are very fond of putting a large blob where they want the hole, but they will need to know the exact point where to place the drill bit.) If the hole needs to be in the centre of the wood, the children should be encouraged to measure the wood in order to find the centre, rather than guess (figure 6).

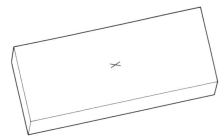

Figure 6 Marking the position to drill

The wood must be fixed to the table or bench in some way – either with a G-cramp or in a vice – as it is dangerous to hold wood while it is being drilled.

Using a G-cramp

A thick piece of scrap wood should be placed underneath the wood to be drilled to protect the table. The hand drill should be held vertically in the left hand and the handle turned in a clockwise direction with the right hand. (This is true for both right and left-handed people.) Some slight downward pressure can be exerted but the speed of rotation of the drill is more important in order to cut a clean hole (figure 7).

Children will find it difficult to hold the drill steady with one hand while turning vigorously with the other. They will also have difficulty in

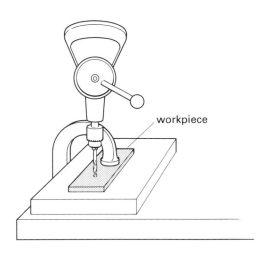

Figure 7 Drilling a workpiece held by a G-cramp

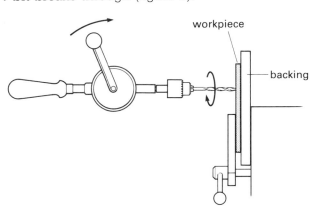

Figure 8 Drilling a workpiece held in a vice

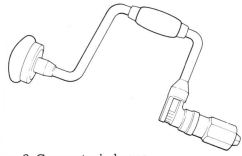

Figure 9 Carpenter's brace

keeping the drill vertical. It may be worth allowing them to practise using only the stronger drill bits, say 3 mm and upwards.

Using a vice

This time the wood is held vertically while the operator drills horizontally. It is not essential to have a piece of scrap wood behind the workpiece in this case, though its presence will avoid the hole splitting at the back as the drill bit breaks through (figure 8).

The children will find it difficult to keep the drill level, but they can be aided by a partner who crouches down until the drill is at eye level and tells the operator when the drill is out of alignment.

Hand drills or twist drills will accept bits up to 6 mm ($\frac{1}{4}$ inch) in diameter. To make larger holes a carpenter's brace could be used (figure 9). This accepts drill bits up to 12 mm ($\frac{1}{2}$ inch) in diameter or auger bits for making even larger holes. Young children, however, may find these braces heavy and awkward to use, so perhaps their introduction should be delayed until they have some mastery of the smaller hand drill.

Adding a handle to the wheel

In order for the wheel to be turned smoothly it will need a handle. Two ideas for doing this are illustrated in figure 10.

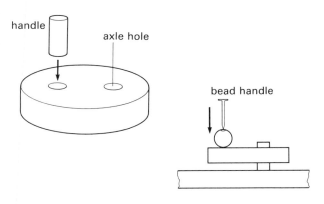

Figure 10 Two suggestions for handles

Securing the wheel

Figure 11 illustrates two methods of keeping the wheel on its axle.

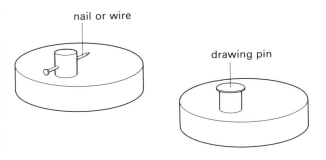

Figure 11 Keeping a wheel on a dowel axle

Models with a lever

Some of the children's models will have a lever that is operated by the wheel. This would need to be hinged or pivoted at some point on the body of the model. The pivot could be a short length of dowel, a nail or perhaps a screw (figure 12).

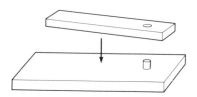

Drill a small hole
in the moving part
to take the screw or nail

Figure 12 Suggestions for attaching the lever

It would help the children a great deal and not influence their design too much if they were shown working examples of these wheel and lever mechanisms as you talk about them. They would take only a while to make up and give you the chance to practise your craft skills.

Wheel and lever connection

The wheel could connect with the lever in two ways, depending on the relative sizes and positions of the model parts. Figure 13 illustrates these.

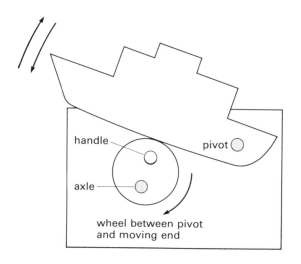

handle

pivot

axle

wheel between pivot
and moving end

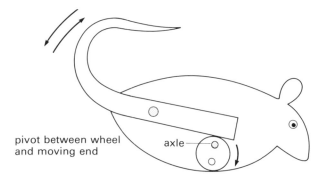

pivot between wheel
and moving end

axle

Figure 13 Two arrangements for connecting the wheel to the lever

Models which stand up

The children will probably want their model to stand up, so they will need to think of simple methods of support. Figure 14 shows some examples of how this might be achieved.

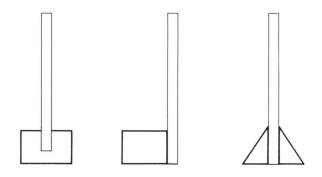

Figure 14 Supporting a standing model

Overcoming difficulties

The following situations may help to illustrate some of the difficulties that might be encountered. Some practical solutions to these are offered.

Sarah's dragon

Sarah had been intrigued by the story of St George and the dragon and so the suggestion that someone had made about animals with moving heads had set off a train of thought.

Her idea was to cut a dragon profile from fairly thin wood and have a moving upper jaw worked by a wheel at the back (figure 15). When Sarah cut her model idea from card,

Figure 15 Sarah's drawings

she forgot to include a lever on the upper jaw and so had to glue this piece on later. She had also underestimated the area of card needed for the pivot, so a weak point developed. All these initial problems, however, were overcome in a matter of minutes by recutting the upper jaws and lever as one piece (figure 16).

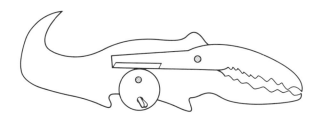

Figure 16 Sarah's card mock-up

Sarah's final model didn't overcome the problem of the thickness of the wood – the upper jaw was set back from the lower one – but this didn't seem important to her.

Figure 17 Sarah's finished dragon

John's coffin

At first John was happy to have a rectangular base with another rectangle for the lid, which opened slowly as the wheel was turned. With his teacher's help, John worked out how to have the lid flush with the base by glueing a fabric hinge on one end. The wheel would rub on a small wood strip glued to the back of the lid (figure 18). She also encouraged him to make a more interesting shape for the box.

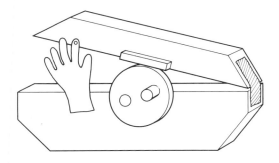

Figure 18 John's finished coffin

As John progressed with the construction of his coffin, he accumulated further ideas that he had not initially put on his design drawing. He decided to add a fabric hand to the lid. This hung down as the lid opened and appeared to be opening it. Later, a spider, made of wire, was seen hanging from the end of the lid! The coffin was finally 'decorated' with nail heads and felt tip spider's webs.

Sabrina's see-saw

Sabrina decided to use the idea that her wheel could push a rod up and down, which in turn would rock a see-saw. Figure 19 shows her design drawing.

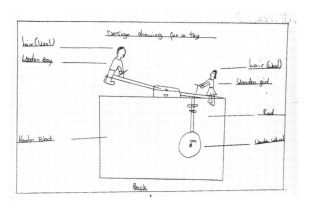

Figure 19 Sabrina's design drawing

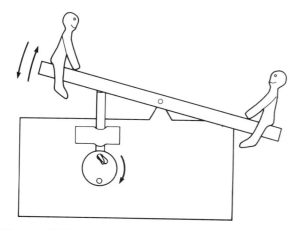

Figure 20 Sabrina's card mock-up

Her card model (figure 20) was flat but she was determined to make a life-like scale model. The special pivot needed for the centre of the three-dimensional see-saw gave her teacher something to think about. She discussed it with Sabrina.

'What kind of things would make a hinge at the middle of the see-saw – a door hinge, a piece of strong cloth glued into position, a piece of flexible plastic stapled into place?'

Sabrina decided a piece of tough leather would be best because she could fix that herself (figure 21). She was allowed to varnish her model to give an attractive finish but she had to be careful not to get the moving parts stuck together. The finished model had two clothes peg children riding on the see-saw. They were dressed in clothes that Sabrina had made at home during the weekend.

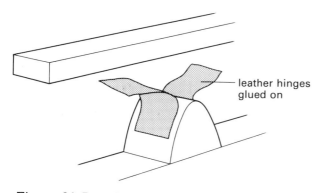

leather hinges glued on

Figure 21 Details of Sabrina's hinge

Karla's boat at sea

Karla wanted a boat sinking at sea. All we were to see was half of the stricken boat as it floundered in the waves (figure 22).

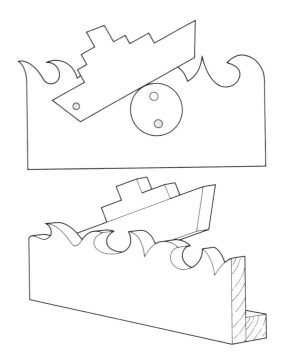

Figure 22 Karla's boat

Karla had to remember how to use the coping saw when it came to cutting the waves but the softwood she was using was easy to cut and not too thick. She made a stand for her model from a simple block of wood glued to the back of the 'ocean' (figure 22).

Karla painted her sea and boat with school water paints and when those were dry, she gave the model a coat of varnish.

Carol's clown

Carol still had fond memories of the trip to the circus in the first year, so she made a clown bobbing up over a wall (figure 23). There were

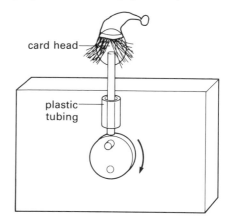

card head

plastic tubing

Figure 23 Carol's clown

problems with this model though, because the rod kept getting jammed on the rough exterior of the wheel. This was finally solved by using a smaller wheel and fixing a plastic 'tyre' to it with a special glue suitable for plastics.

Carol didn't like using varnish so she was shown how to rub linseed oil into the wood parts of her model with a small piece of cloth. Carol had sanded her model carefully, so she was pleased when the linseed oil showed up the wood grain so well.

Evaluating the finished models

Some time should be given to evaluating the models when they are finished. These points should be considered either with individuals or in a group discussion:

- Does the moving part of the toy move smoothly?

- Is the movement sufficiently large?

- Does the toy look attractive?

- Is it safe to play with?

- Was sufficient time available to complete the project?

- If there were more time, what improvements could be made?

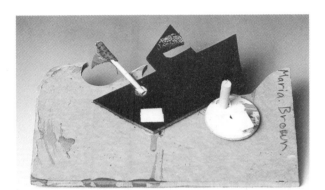

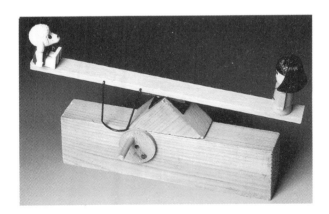

Figure 24 Some entertaining outcomes

Similar projects

Design and make a toy that has one or two moving parts that are levers. The moving parts should be worked by pulling a string at the back of the model.

Figure 25 illustrates two examples of the types of model the children might produce.

Design and make some play apparatus for a pet gerbil or hamster. The apparatus must fit comfortably inside the cage and be safe to use. Figure 26 illustrates some examples.

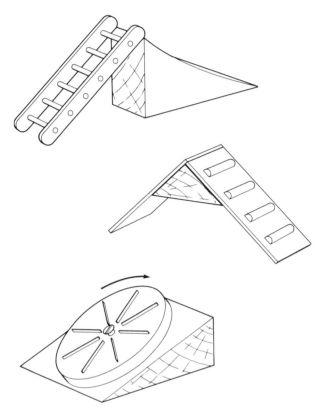

Figure 26 Play apparatus for a pet rodent

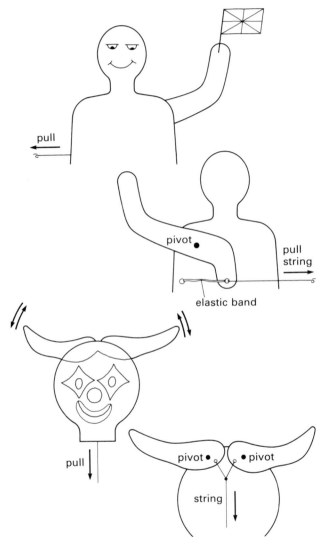

Figure 25 String-and-lever arrangements

Research

Measure the cage and its door to find the maximum dimensions for the model.

Observe the gerbil's habits. What kind of exercise does it enjoy?

Consider playground apparatus made for children.

Find out about bearings to enable the wheel to run smoothly.

ABOUT . . .

The eccentric wheel

When an eccentric wheel is turning, it moves from one extreme to the other: full up to full down.

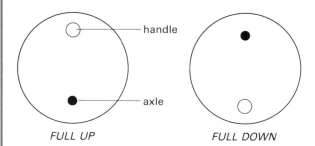

FULL UP   *FULL DOWN*

Children could be asked to say how they think this movement could be made greater or less. The position of the axle is significant here, assuming we keep the size of the wheel the same.

A will move up and down more than **B**.

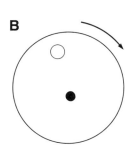

Naturally, a larger wheel will produce a larger movement if we keep the axle in the same position – say 1 cm from the centre.

C will move up and down more than **D**.

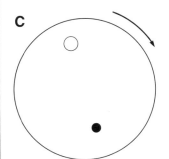
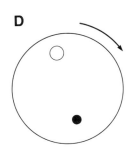

The lever

The moving part of a model can be a simple lever moved by a wheel pushing on one end. The distance through which the other end moves can be changed by altering the position of the pivot.

These teeth

will move more than these.

These teeth

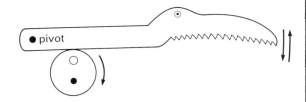

will move more than these.

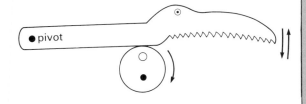

5 Propeller-driven vehicles

SUMMARY

The task
Design and make a vehicle that is driven by a propeller powered by an elastic band. The chassis of the vehicle must be constructed using a wood-strip and card framework. Your vehicle should be designed to go as far as possible on 15 winds of the propeller.

This project will introduce children to a simple and effective method for constructing a strong framework. Once a framework has been constructed to a suitable shape, it can then be used for a large number of technological projects ranging from vehicle chassis to bridges and cranes. In addition to this valuable skill, the children will have the chance to explore the use of propellers for motive power. There will be less reliance on woodworking skills in this project and a greater concentration on technical principles.

This topic can be easily introduced into the classroom in a number of ways. Vehicles could be constructed as part of a theme on transport, movement or air. Equally, they could provide the basis for a school technology competition.

As long as desk tops are protected, this project can be run in an ordinary classroom. However, certain inexpensive items will have to be supplied to the children, such as elastic bands, beads, small propellers and wheels. Plastic propellers can be obtained from a number of commercial suppliers. They range in size from about 8 to 15 cm in diameter and can be either two or three-bladed. Wheels are also commercially available and come in many sizes from 2 cm in diameter upwards. Plastic 'balloon' wheels or pre-cut wooden ones are available, too. It is possible, however, to make your own wheels from container lids or even stiff card, but there may be difficulties with fixing these securely to the axle. See also the paragraph on wheels on page 45.

THE TASK
Design and make a vehicle that is driven by a propeller powered by an elastic band. The chassis of the vehicle must be constructed using a wood-strip and card framework. Your vehicle should be designed to go as far as possible on 15 winds of the propeller.

The initial research for this project will need to be centred on the skill of constructing a wooden frame for the chassis of the vehicle. Further investigations will be required later when different types of propeller are put on trial.

Constructing a wood-strip and card framework

Equipment needed

- Square section strips of softwood.
  These can be cut to length by the children.
  Any section from 0.5 cm square to 1 cm
  square will do, but all the strips should have
  the same dimensions in cross-section. They
  can be obtained cheaply either from a
  woodyard or from educational suppliers.

- Reasonably stiff card and glue.

Making a right-angled joint

Cut out a corner-plate from card, measuring
about 3 cm × 3 cm (figure 1). Then cut some
wood strips to length using a saw and bench
hook, as shown in figure 2.

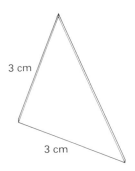

3 cm

3 cm

Figure 1 Card corner-plate

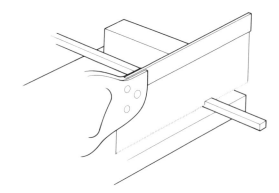

Figure 2 Cutting wood strips to length

Lay them in position and glue a card corner-
plate over them for reinforcement. Use any
suitable wood glue (figure 3). This joint may be
reinforced by glueing a second card corner-
plate on the other side (figure 4).

Figure 3 Reinforcing the corner

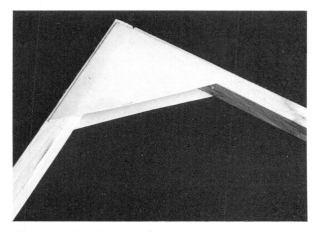

Figure 4 Further reinforcement

For joints which are not at right angles, the
card will need to be cut to suit the angle
required. Notice that there is no need to glue
the pieces of wood to each other (figure 5).

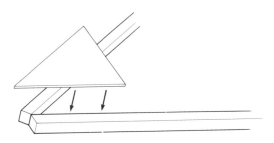

Figure 5 Acute-angled joint

Right-angled card corner-plates can be
conveniently made by cutting lots of them from
a card rectangle (figure 6).

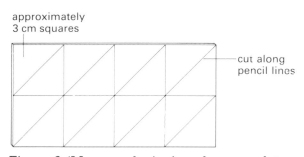

approximately
3 cm squares

cut along
pencil lines

Figure 6 'Mass-producing' card corner-plates

PVA adhesive is suitable for this work and can be made to dry quickly to form a strong working joint by rubbing in a layer of adhesive on both surfaces to be glued. Rub the adhesive with a finger until it starts to become tacky then bring both surfaces together and hold them tightly for a few seconds to produce an immediate bond.

Practising the technique

It is worth asking the children to work through a short exercise to allow them to practise this technique. Ask them to build a triangular prism to the dimensions you give them. They will need to be able to make both right-angled and acute-angled corner joints and to measure and cut the short sections of wood carefully. You may find the worksheet opposite helpful here.

Design considerations

The children will need to consider the following points before they make any final decisions about their model.

- The chassis will need to be strong enough to take the compressive force exerted by the twisted elastic band as well as holding the wheels.

- The vehicle should be as light as possible to allow it to travel as far as possible.

- At least three wheels will be needed for the vehicle.

- The propeller will need to be held clear of the ground. There should also be enough clearance to fit a larger propeller later.

- One end of the elastic band will need to be firmly anchored to the edge of the chassis.

- Will the propeller be able to push from the back as well as pull from the front?

- The propeller will need a shaft. What could this be made from? A straightened paperclip, perhaps?

- The propeller must be free to spin rapidly, so it will need a bearing of some kind. A bead, perhaps?

The children will need to be shown the propeller mechanism so that they have some idea of the design requirements for the vehicle.

This must be done without influencing where and how they will position the propeller on the vehicle. The arrangement in figure 7 would be a suitable model to show them. If you have an elastic band propelled aeroplane, then this would be a useful model to show the children. It could be released to run along the table without actually taking off, thus giving them some idea how a propeller works.

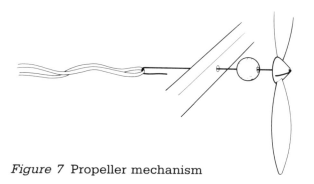

Figure 7 Propeller mechanism

Designing the chassis

Children will probably find it difficult to draw their chassis directly from their imagination. The following exercise, therefore, might help. Ask the children to begin by making a full-sized model of their proposed chassis using art straws. They will inevitably find it easier to make their drawings using this straw model.

Fixing straws together

Figure 8 illustrates how a joint may be made between three straws using pipe cleaners. Two pipe cleaners are inserted into one end of each straw. This makes a strong joint which can then be carefully bent into the shape required. Additional straws can be added to any joint by pulling one straw away from its two pipe

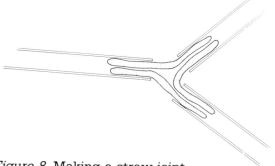

Figure 8 Making a straw joint

Worksheet

Making a Strong Frame

Remember to make the corners of your frame like this.

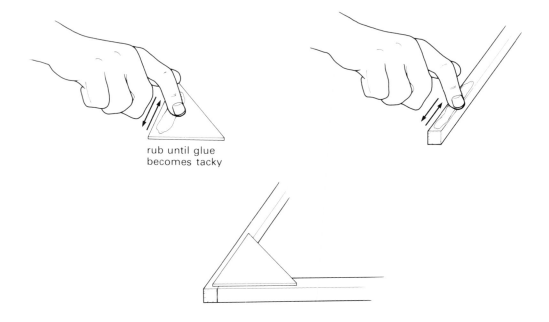

rub until glue
becomes tacky

Now build a frame exactly this size.

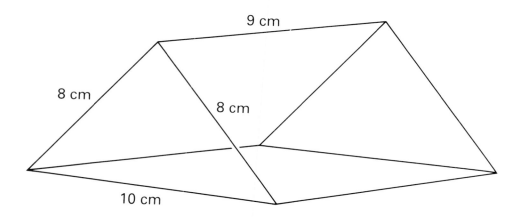

9 cm

8 cm

8 cm

10 cm

You will need to measure and cut your wood strips carefully.

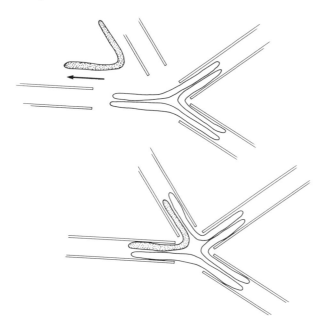

Figure 9 Adding more straws to the joint

cleaners, inserting one of these pipe cleaners into the new straw along with a new pipe cleaner, and reassembling the joint, as shown in figure 9.

Once the children have mastered this technique, discuss with them the different kinds of plan view their chassis could have. These are best sketched on the blackboard as the children suggest them. Figure 10 shows the variations in the plan view of the chassis that the children might suggest.

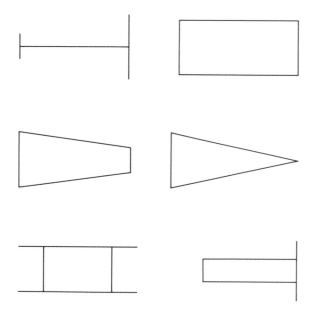

Figure 10 **Variations on the plan view of the chassis**

Next, the children will need to think about supporting the propeller high enough so that it does not strike the ground as it rotates. A framework will need to be built up from the horizontal part of the chassis, as illustrated in figure 11.

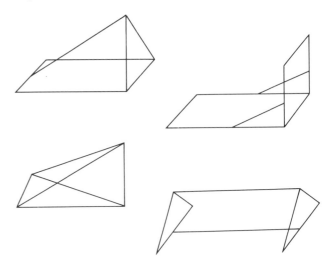

Figure 11 **Four configurations of framework to support the propeller**

The children will now have enough information to build their straw mock-up for the chassis. You might decide, however, to explain how the wheels can be attached to the wooden chassis before they do this.

Figure 12 Building a straw model

Fixing wheels to axles

Axles could be made from straight lengths of wire, such as welding wire or old coat hangers, or from small-sectioned dowel, e.g. 6 mm ($\frac{1}{4}$ inch) or less. Wire which can be cut and shaped with pliers is probably more effective than dowel. The method by which the axle is to be fixed to the wheel will depend on the hole that is available in the wheel. If the wheel can be jammed tightly on to the axle, then this will work well. However, if the axle is slightly smaller than the hole in the wheel, then wrap some sticky tape round the axle until it fits tightly in the wheel. With this arrangement the axle will move with the wheel. The alternative is to have the wheel free on the axle, in which case some arrangement will have to be made to prevent the wheel from sliding off. Figure 13 demonstrates two ways which a wheel can be mounted on an axle.

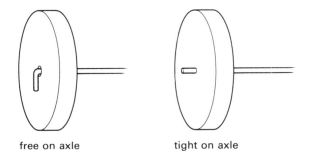

free on axle   tight on axle

Figure 13 **Holding a wheel on its axle**

If the wheels are to be fixed rigidly to the axles, then the axles will need to be able to run freely through holes in the chassis. This can be done either by drilling holes through the wood strips or glueing to the chassis stiff card brackets in which holes have been punched. Children will find it difficult to align the holes, so the card bracket method is to be recommended. These can be slid into position while the glue is still wet. The brackets should be as rigid as possible, so give the children the thickest card you can find. Clean holes can be cut in the brackets with a heavy duty hole punch. If PVA adhesive is not strong enough to hold the bracket, use a hot glue gun. Figure 14 demonstrates how card brackets can be used to fit the axles to the chassis.

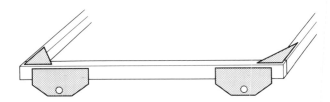

Figure 14 **Card brackets to hold the axles**

Design drawings

With their straw frames in front of them, the children will find that they can begin by drawing a plan view of the chassis and then add the side view afterwards. Remind them that they are not drawing the straw model but the final wood-strip model. They will therefore need to show the width of the wood strips in their diagrams as well as the card corner-plates, if possible. When they have done this, the propeller and elastic band arrangement can be drawn in. This should include a wire shaft running through the propeller, a bead or similar bearing, and a firm support for this on the chassis (figure 11).

The children could mark the lengths of the individual wood strips on their drawings to help them when they get to the construction stage. Encourage the children to shade their drawings to give them a polished finish. Figure 15 shows a typical design drawing that might be expected.

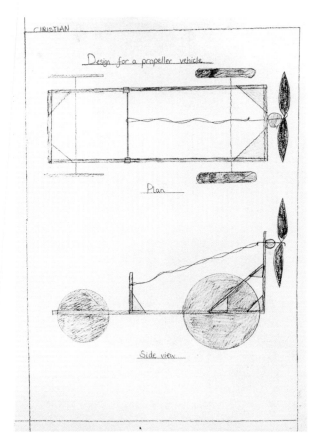

Figure 15 **Typical design drawing for a vehicle**

Making the vehicles

When construction begins, the children will need a ready supply of wood strips, card and adhesive. They will need to use bench hooks, saws, and glasspaper for smoothing the ragged ends of the wood strips. Joints on the chassis should be allowed to harden before any great pressure is put on them. It is surprising how much stronger they become after leaving them overnight.

Technical hitches

The following examples are some of the problems that might arise in a project of this nature along with some suggestions for their solution.

Children abandon the plans they have drawn and begin making a model which is much smaller

If the model is too short, there will not be enough room to hold the elastic band and propeller arrangement. If the band is too short it will not take enough winds. If it is too slack at the beginning it will be difficult to wind up. A shortened model will be more prone to instability in that it may topple over or veer to one side. A length of 15 cm or more would be reasonable.

The vehicle turns to one side as it moves forward

The axles are not parallel to each other. Either the card brackets must be moved in relation to each other or a new hole will have to be punched in one of them. Alternatively, the wheels may not be at right-angles to the axles, so they will have to be straightened.

The support for the propeller is not strong enough

When the elastic band is wound up, a strong pull is generated between the propeller support and the point at which the elastic is anchored at the other end of the chassis. A support consisting of a single wood-strip post, for instance, will almost certainly be pulled over, so a strengthening structure will need to be built.

The propeller doesn't turn smoothly and therefore fast enough to pull the vehicle along

This is usually because the propeller shaft is not straight or because a part of the mechanism catches on the chassis. Sometimes just a small adjustment to the shaft will make a large difference to performance.

The vehicle doesn't move forwards when the propeller is released

This is obviously very disappointing when so much effort has gone into making the model but it is likely to happen two out of three times on the first attempt. There are many solutions to this problem.

- Is the propeller large enough for the job? Is it the right shape? (Improvement of propeller design is discussed later.)
- Make sure the vehicle runs smoothly with a small push across the table. If not, check that the axles and wheels spin freely when the vehicle is picked up.
- Try giving the propeller more winds. Just a little more energy stored in the elastic band will make quite a difference.
- Add another elastic band if the one currently being used is too weak.
- Is the propeller pointing forward enough or does it resemble a helicopter rotor blade?
- Does the elastic band catch on the chassis as it unwinds?
- Is the vehicle too heavy?
- Is the surface it is running on smooth enough? Floor tiles or a large, smooth table are better than a carpet.

Ideas that work well

The following ideas have worked well in practice. They are illustrated here as examples for the teacher to have in mind. Care must be taken, however, to accept the children's own ideas, even if they will quite obviously be less effective. Our intention is not that children make models that are sure to work well, copied from our own designs, but that they learn to have confidence in their own ideas while making models with a certain degree of success.

'Tentmobile'

The children who have made models similar to the one illustrated in figure 16 will have understood how to be efficient in their use of wood. They will have used triangles as part of their design, giving it added strength while using the minimum of materials. A strong frame will have been constructed which will be able to take the strain of the twisted elastic band.

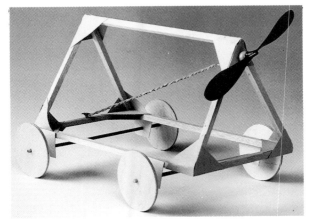

Figure 16 'Tentmobile'

Lightest model

The pair who built this model tried to use the smallest number of strips so that their model was as light as possible. Only five wood strips have been used and yet all the essential features are there: one frame to hold the wheels and one to hold the propeller. Special brackets have been developed to hold the axles (figure 17).

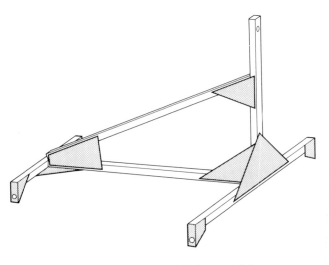

Figure 17 Structure for a light model

Three-wheeler

The model in the shape of a tetrahedron uses only three wheels (figure 18). Furthermore it has the propeller at the back.

Figure 18 Three-wheeler with 'pusher' propeller

Evaluation: testing and improving

If you have given the children the small propellers designed for model aircraft or high speed motors, then the chances are that they will not work very efficiently on some of the more cumbersome vehicles. This we have done on purpose! An important part of the process of solving problems is the testing and improving stage. Here we expect the model to be put through trials, its weaknesses analysed and improvements made. The children may need some assistance with analysing the drawbacks of their small propellers.

Ask the children how they think the vehicle moves forward. If they have worked on paddle boats (Chapter 3), they may be able to explain that air is pushed backwards by the propeller so that the vehicle moves forward. They may be able to point out that the propeller appears to twist through the air as a corkscrew twists through a cork or a bolt through a nut.

Ask them to describe how more air could be pushed backwards or how the propeller could get a better grip on the air as it screws through it. The answer you are looking for would be a bigger propeller.

Then ask what would stop us from using a propeller as big as the table. Hopefully they

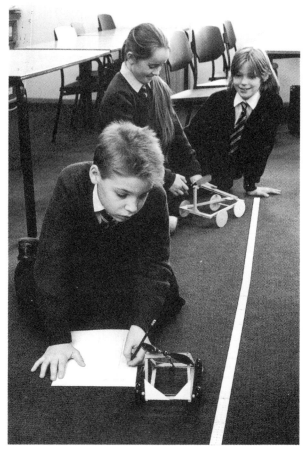

Figure 19 Testing propeller-driven models

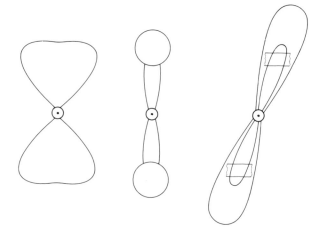

Figure 20 Examples of redesigned propellers

should come up with the solution that there is not enough room to hold it on the chassis and that, anyway, the vehicle would collapse under the weight.

So, a bigger propeller is a good thing up to a limit.

If you now show the children how to make their propeller bigger, they can go away and experiment with different designs.

Redesigning the propeller

A larger propeller means one with a larger area, or at least a redistribution of area. With this in mind, encourage the children to try not only enlarged versions of their present propeller but also new shapes and even more blades. This can be done easily by cutting thin plastic shapes from containers and fixing them to the existing blades with sticky tape. These can easily be removed and replaced during the trials (figure 20).

The children will find that a propeller with a larger area makes a significant difference to the performance of the vehicle. The blades will

tend to rotate more slowly than before as a greater amount of air is encountered but the vehicle can be expected to move gracefully across the room and out of the door if allowed to.

Similar projects

Project 1

Design and make a vehicle that moves using the energy of a falling weight. The chassis can be constructed in a similar way to that used in the propeller-driven vehicle.

Research

The children can best understand how a falling weight can drive the wheels of a vehicle by constructing the simple apparatus shown in figure 21.

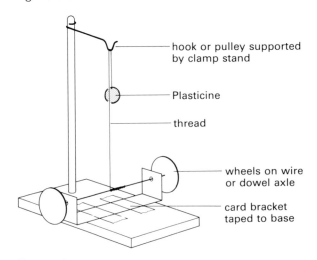

Figure 21 Apparatus to demonstrate the falling-weight principle

Making the vehicle

The chassis could be of a similar construction to those already discussed with the addition of a tower to hold the pulley for the falling weight. One possible solution is illustrated in figure 22.

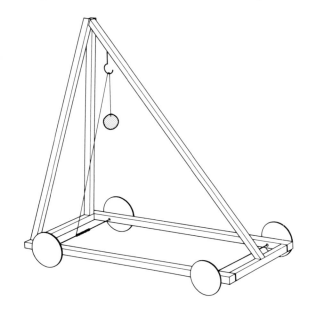

Figure 22 Vehicle powered by a falling weight

Variations in the speed and distance travelled can be achieved by changing the diameter of the axle, changing the diameter of the wheels, overcoming friction in the mechanism, or using a heavier weight up to an optimum size.

Note that in this project the wheels must be fixed firmly to the axles. The axles can be given greater diameters by wrapping sticky tape around them or winding on a quantity of thread. An interesting gearing system could be developed by creating sections of different diameter on the axle.

Project 2

Design and make a vehicle that is driven by the energy in a stretched elastic band. The elastic band must be wound around one axle of the vehicle thus stretching its remaining length.

The drive principle is shown in figure 23. The points made about axles and gearing in the challenge above apply equally to this project.

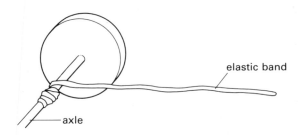

Figure 23 Driving wheels by the energy stored in an elastic band

The points made in Chapter 3 concerning energy changes and action and reaction apply equally to a propeller-driven vehicle.

Wheels and axles

Much of the technology concerned with wheels and axles has been discussed already. The wheels must be able to spin freely and must be aligned correctly. Friction is the main enemy here and must be overcome as much as possible. Lubricants such as oil, butter or soap may be used on the axles to improve running.

The propeller and its mechanism

As explained earlier, a propeller slices through air in the same way a screw turns into wood. At the beginning, when the vehicle is not moving, the air is thrown backwards, but as motion is taken up this happens less. If the blades of the propeller are at a shallow angle or pitch (see figure below) then they will not move as far forward in one turn as they would if they were more sharply angled. Too sharp an angle, however, will mean that the blades meet more air resistance as they spin round and so they will not pick up sufficient speed. Getting the pitch right on a propeller is very important.

The pitch of each blade may vary on a commercially produced propeller. It is usually greater near the centre of the propeller than at the blade's extremity. It is made this way because the tip of the blade moves faster than the centre and therefore needs to slice through the air more effectively.

Reducing friction

The bead which acts as a bearing between the propeller and the chassis reduces friction by reducing the area of contact between the moving parts. It also holds the propeller away from the chassis. In some cases two beads may be necessary. As with the wheels and axles, lubricants may be used to good effect on the bead.

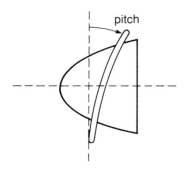

pitch

6 Electrical switches

SUMMARY

The tasks

1 Make a switch that will trigger a burglar alarm. The switch should work when a door has just been opened.

2 Make a switch that operates when the level of water in a container reaches a certain level. You may choose your own container and the level to which it must be filled.

3 Make a moving switch that makes a bulb flash.

4 Make a switch that cuts out when it is pushed. The switch could be fixed to the front of an electrically driven vehicle so that it turns off the motor when the vehicle hits an obstacle.

Equipment and general organisation

Not all design and technology projects need to involve making models in resistant materials and not all projects need to be long-term ones. The following set of problems may require some simple construction in card or plastic but they are designed to last for only an hour or two each. The four separate problems share a common theme – electrical switches – but could easily be taken as individual tasks that complement some topic work currently being undertaken. Children who know nothing about batteries and bulbs will find this project a stimulating introduction to them. Alternatively, these series of problems will provide an added stimulus to those children who have been introduced to electrical circuits in a previous science topic.

The equipment used is fairly simple but it will need to be stored and distributed carefully so that components are not lost. It may be that the equipment has to be shared with another class, so the projects have been designed to be dismantled and packed away at the end of each working session.

Equipment and general organisation

Batteries

It is essential that the batteries used for these projects can be easily connected to other components. Some batteries, such as the 4.5 volt 'flat' batteries, have brass strip connectors that paperclips or crocodile clips can be fixed to while others, such as the large torch batteries (HP2), need to be held in a suitably-sized holder.

Torch batteries are often sold in a made-to-measure box. This might contain 25 or 30 batteries. If you keep the batteries stored in this box then it will be easier to see if one or more is missing.

If you can afford them, flag cells (Ever Ready R40) are a useful alternative to the awkward torch batteries. These are large, cylindrical and have two useful screw terminals on top. They may also turn out to be more economical in the long run since they have a long life.

Battery holders

There are a variety of battery holders commercially available for HP2 cells, from the oversized Worcester Circuit Boards to small plastic single or double-cell holders (figure 1 and 2). If leads with crocodile clips at each end are used, these can be clipped to the battery holder terminals and then connected to light bulbs and switches.

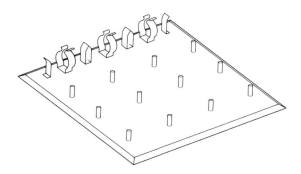

Figure 1 Worcester Circuit Board

Figure 2 Simple plastic battery holder

Worcester Circuit Boards can be stacked and transported on a trolley, while the smaller holders can be stored in a made-to-measure box.

Crocodile connectors

A simple way of connecting components is to use a crocodile connector, i.e. a lead with a crocodile clip at each end (figure 3).

Figure 3 A crocodile connector

Commercially produced circuit boards may have alternative ways of making electrical connections, usually using a spring system, but at some time crocodile connectors will be useful.

Crocodile connectors need to be stored carefully because they can easily get into a tangled mess. One way of doing this is to use two parallel strips between which each connector is clipped. This might take the form of a specially made wooden frame or simply a tough card box that is long and narrow (figure 4).

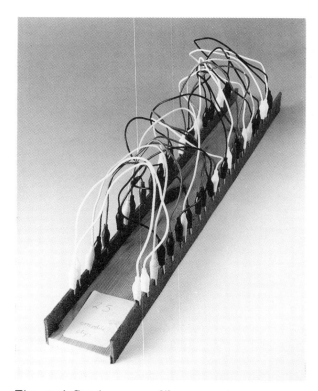

Figure 4 Storing crocodile connectors

Light bulbs

A variety of bulbs can be purchased and it is important to choose the correct rating for a particular project. In general, two 1.5 volt batteries will be used so a 3.5 volt bulb would be suitable. (Choose a 4.5 or 6 volt bulb for use with a 'flat' battery.) The current rating in amps is also marked on the bulb. If you want a brighter bulb choose a high current rating. Warn the children that if they try to use three HP2 batteries with one bulb then they are likely to blow it. All bulbs will blow at some time anyway, so it is a good idea to have a number of spares ready.

Light bulb holders

A light bulb is held in a commercially available holder, to which crocodile clips can be fixed. Alternatively, the holder may attach to pegs on a circuit board, to which in turn crocodile clips can be attached (figure 5).

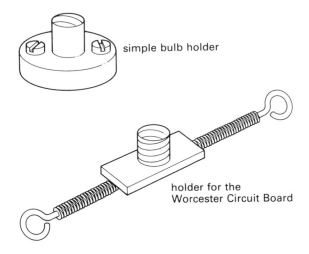

simple bulb holder

holder for the
Worcester Circuit Board

Figure 5 Light bulb holders

Storing bulbs and holders

Bulbs are best stored in their holders, which can then be kept in some kind of rack such as the ones illustrated in figures 6 and 7.

nails in board

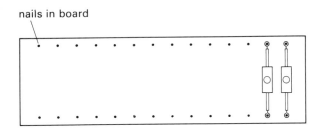

Figure 6 Storage rack for the Worcester Circuit Board bulb holder

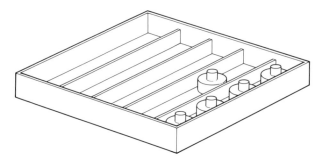

Figure 7 Storage rack for simple bulb holder

Research

The research for this project is in two parts: (i) an introduction to making an electrical circuit and (ii) making various switches. The introduction here is based on the HP2 torch battery. If you are using another type of battery some adaptation will be required.

Making a circuit

Give each child a battery (HP2 torch battery), a bulb and a length of plastic insulated wire with the ends bared. Ask the children to use just these components to light the bulb. Encourage them to find as many different ways as possible of getting the bulb to light and then choose an opportune moment to mention that there are four ways of doing this (figure 8).

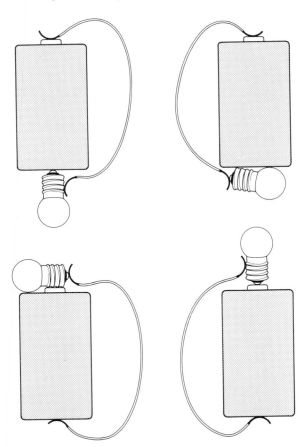

Figure 8 Four ways of making a bulb light up

The children will see that the bulb lights up only when the components make a 'circle' or circuit. They can now see clearly what it is that stops the electricity flowing – a break in the circuit – and this will lead on to thinking about electrical switches.

Electrical switches

Figure 9 Using a Worcester Circuit Board

Show the children how to set up a simple circuit using more appropriate components such as battery holders, crocodile clips and bulb holders. Some may quickly complain that their circuit does not work, which may be for a variety of reasons. Since part of this work is about analysing and solving minor technical problems, this is probably a good time to teach the children how to find out what is wrong with a circuit and how to correct it themselves.

The information sheet opposite could be given to children as a reminder that it is they who are in charge of putting faulty circuits right! You will need to provide some simple tools, such as small electrical screwdrivers, a pair of pliers, wire strippers and a reel of insulating tape. Faulty components should be placed in a tray or box ready to be repaired or discarded after the lesson.

Making switches

The children could continue their research by learning how to make their own electrical switches. First, let the children try some commercially available switches in the circuits they have made. If they are given the appropriate tools, they could take these apart to see how they work. They will find that commercially available switches have metal components including springs and screw terminals. You can show them now how to make their own switches using card, plastic and aluminium foil.

Card or plastic strips can easily be cut to shape with scissors and then covered in foil. Neat holes can be cut in these components

using a hole punch and smaller ones made with compasses or a drawing pin (figure 10).

These components can then be fixed to baseboards of stiff card with brass paper fasteners. If ready-cut wooden blocks are available, drawing pins can be used for fixing.

Connecting leads can be made on a base board by cutting and glueing strips of

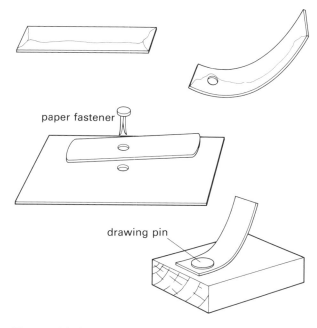

Figure 10 Switch components made from card or flexible plastic pieces covered in aluminium foil

aluminium foil. These leads can be run to the edge of the board so that crocodile connectors can join the switch to the rest of the circuit (figure 11).

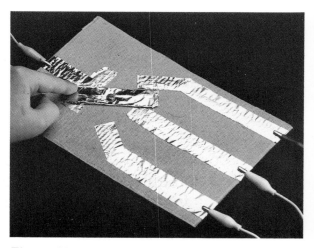

Figure 11 Aluminium foil leads arranged as on a huge printed-circuit board.

Trouble shooting with electrical circuits

Check all the components you are going to use by building a circuit to light a bulb. If the bulb doesn't light, you must find the fault. Try the following steps for yourself. It is usually best to test your components in the order given below.

Fault	*Remedy*
Poor electrical contact	Turn batteries in their holders or wiggle them about. Move crocodile connectors and press them firmly into position. Screw bulb firmly into holder. Tighten any loose screws on crocodile clips and bulb holders.
Faulty bulb	Replace bulb. Put faulty one in Faulty Equipment Tray.
Dead battery	Replace battery. Put faulty one in Faulty Equipment Tray.
Batteries incorrectly connected	Turn one battery round so that negative is connected to positive.
Faulty connector	Tighten screw on each crocodile clip or replace connector. Put faulty connector in Faulty Equipment Tray.
Faulty bulb holder	Tighten screws and check wiring or replace with another. Put faulty holder in Faulty Equipment Tray.

If you have tried all the steps above and your circuit still doesn't work, then it is just possible you have *two* pieces of faulty equipment. Test each of your components on a friend's circuit that you know is working.

Remember, it is up to you.

Having shown the children the principles of switch making, allow them to practise by working through the worksheet opposite.

Burglar alarm

THE TASK
Make a switch that will trigger a burglar alarm. The switch should work when a door has just been opened. Make a card model of the doorway and build your switch into this as neatly as you can. At first your alarm will be a light bulb but successful models can be connected to an electric bell or buzzer.

In asking the group to illuminate a light bulb as the alarm, you can ensure a fairly quiet classroom and also allow for the fact that there may be only a limited number of bells and buzzers in stock. You could have one circuit arranged on your desk with an alarm bell or buzzer in it and eventually the children can bring successful models out to it for a realistic trial.

The idea in this problem is to make a 'plug-in' model. The doorway and alarm switch can be made as one unit which can be connected to the battery and bulb circuit with crocodile clips. The clips will conveniently fix to the edge of the card base of the model and connect with the aluminium foil 'leads' which have been stuck to it. This arrangement, of course, will allow the electrical components to be packed away and reassembled for use on another day while model-making is in progress.

Making the doorway

The doorway can be made from card by the children and might form a useful mathematical exercise in measuring, cutting and folding. A piece of corrugated cardboard would form a convenient base while the door can be made out of almost any thickness of card. The measurements given in figure 12 could be sketched on the blackboard.

The door and frame can be glued to the base with PVA adhesive. Fold lines should be scored to achieve a neat fold. The door can be made to swing more freely on its hinge by cutting it away and fixing it back on the frame with sticky tape (figure 13).

When the children have made their door it is

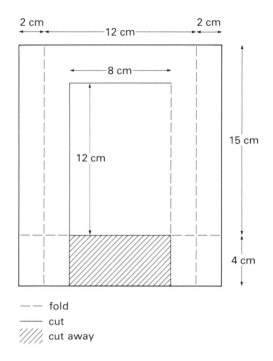

--- fold
— cut
/// cut away

Figure 12 **Suggested measurements for the door and frame**

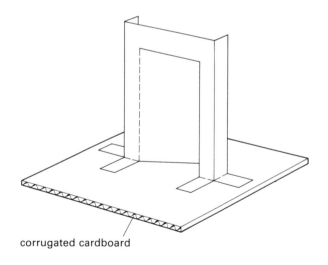

corrugated cardboard

Figure 13 **The complete doorway and base**

up to them to devise a system whereby when the door is just opened an electrical circuit is switched on. The following materials could be made available for the purposes of construction: card, paper, plastic from containers, aluminium foil, thread, string, paperclips, drawing pins, paper fasteners.

The best solutions will be those that are effectively concealed from potential burglars, are neat and tidy and which work every time the door is just opened.

Worksheet

Making Electrical Switches

Make a circuit with two batteries and a bulb ready to take a switch.

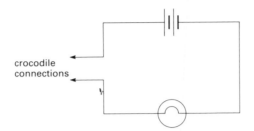

crocodile
connections

Then make each of the following switches and connect them to your circuit to see if they work.

Switch 1

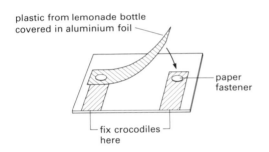

plastic from lemonade bottle covered in aluminium foil

paper fastener

fix crocodiles here

Switch 2

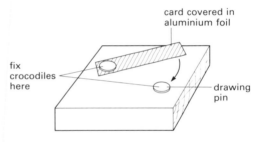

card covered in aluminium foil

fix crocodiles here

drawing pin

Switch 3

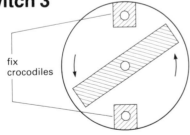

fix crocodiles

Switch 4

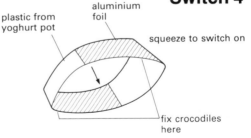

plastic from yoghurt pot

aluminium foil

squeeze to switch on

fix crocodiles here

Switch 5

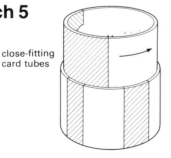

close-fitting card tubes

Switch 6

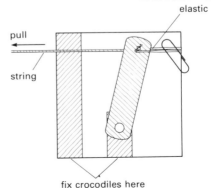

elastic

pull

string

fix crocodiles here

Now make a switch of your own design.
Record your idea in a diagram.

Examples of possible solutions

The solution shown in figure 14, while acceptable, has the disadvantage that it can be seen as the door is opened.

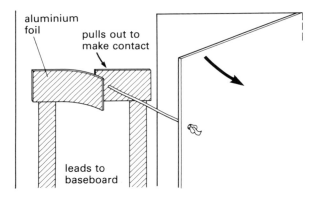

Figure 14 **One way of constructing an alarm switch**

Figure 15 shows a solution which is simpler and will probably work consistently. Notice how the foil leads come to the edge of the baseboard so that the switch can be easily connected to the rest of the circuit using crocodile clips. The doorway is really one large, homemade switch.

Figure 15 Another design for a burglar alarm

Water level alarm

The following problem adds a new dimension to switch-making and will illustrate many practical, everyday uses.

THE TASK
Make a switch that operates when the level of water in a container reaches a certain level.

You may choose your own container and the level to which it must be filled.

An interesting introduction to this problem would be to blindfold a volunteer and ask her to pour a cup of water from a jug. She would have to guess when to stop pouring. Precautions would have to be taken in case of spillage.

This will give the children a clue as to one of the uses for a water level alarm. A device that can be clipped to the side of a tea cup to indicate when it is full of tea would be very useful to a blind or partially sighted person.

A device that indicated when bath water had reached a certain level would be useful to everyone. Every time we flush the toilet and the cistern refills, the water level is controlled by the simple ball-cock. A ball-cock is also employed in the cold water storage tank that most modern homes have in the loft. Could the ball-cock be made into an alarm switch?

The reverse of a rising level indicator can be found in the petrol tank of a car. When the petrol level sinks below a predetermined level, an electrical signal is sent to the dashboard where a needle shows 'near empty'.

The worksheet opposite illustrates the kind of experiences that may help children when they come to design their own water level alarm.

Making the alarm

Once again, extensive use can be made of foil-covered components and the same materials that were provided for the burglar alarm could be made available here. Additional equipment will include: a variety of containers from yoghurt cartons to buckets, cork, wood and polystyrene scraps for floats, Plasticine, sticky tape, bulldog clips, plastic straws, nails and wire.

Problems the children may experience

- When water is poured into the containers it will swirl around and possibly upset the mechanisms the children have set up.
- Children using large buckets or bowls may find it too time consuming to keep emptying and refilling these each time the switch is tested.
- Crocodile clips left in the water will soon corrode. Encourage the children to keep electrical connections well away from the insides of the container.

Marking Water Levels

Build these water level markers and see how they work

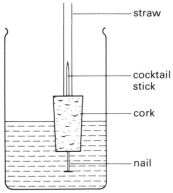

straw

cocktail stick

cork

nail

1 Could the rising straw operate a switch?

2 What will happen to the Plasticine?

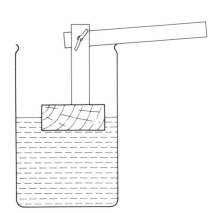

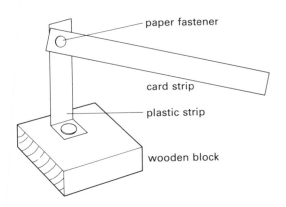

paper fastener

card strip

plastic strip

wooden block

3 Pour the water in gently. Does the lever need a guide to steady it?

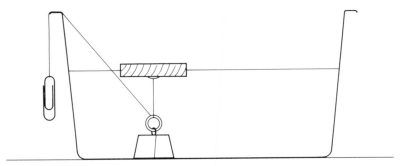

4 Use a large container for this one. What do you think will happen to the paperclip?

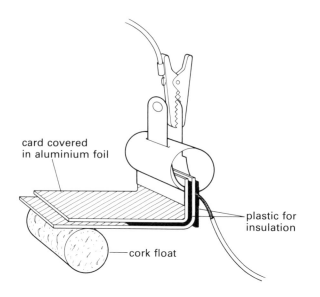

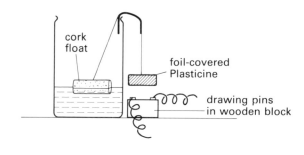

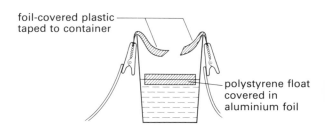

Figure 16 Designs of water level alarm to have in mind

- The switch mechanisms may work inconsistently. A successful switch should work at least three times consecutively.

  The most effective solutions will consist of alarms that can be easily detached from the container, but many children will have done well if they complete one fixed to the container.

Alarms that work well

Figure 16 shows some solutions you could have in mind to prompt those children who are having difficulty getting started.

Switch for a flashing light

THE TASK
Make a moving switch that makes a bulb flash.

Two ideas for a moving switch

- The cotton reel roller (figure 17).
  Hold the stick and the cylinder revolves. Hold the cylinder and the stick swings round. The candle wax bearing gives a controlled, slow revolution.

- The rolling jar (figure 18).
  An empty jar or plastic container will roll

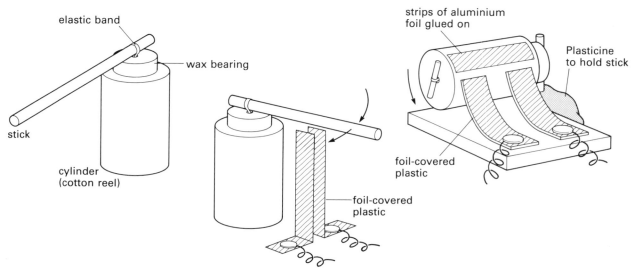

Figure 17 Cotton reel roller switch

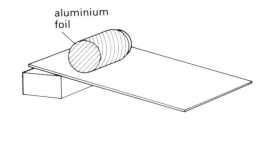

aluminium foil

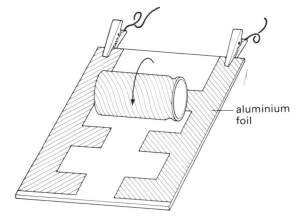

aluminium foil

Figure 18 Rolling jar switch

down quickly and give rapid flashes. If a slower motion is required, then two-thirds fill the jar with viscous wallpaper paste or treacle. Sand, salt or mung beans will have a similar effect.

Pressure switch

This is a switch in which the current must be switched off rather than on. It might be used on the front of an electrically driven toy vehicle, so that when it hits an obstacle the electric motor is turned off.

You will need a toy vehicle with an electric motor, such as a Lego model, and you will also need to get inside the switch so that the leads to it can be reconnected to two crocodile clips. Alternatively, leave the switch in the 'on' position and connect leads from the batteries that can later be joined to complete the circuit. Show the children that if the two crocodile clips are joined, the motor will start and the vehicle can be allowed to crash into the obstacle with its motor still running.

THE TASK
Design and make a switch which cuts out when it is pushed. The switch could be fixed to the front of an electrically driven toy vehicle so that it turns off the motor when the vehicle hits an obstacle.

The device will have to be fixed to the front of the vehicle, perhaps with an elastic band or Blu Tak, and then the crocodile clips will have to be attached to the device. If a Lego vehicle is employed, each child could be supplied with a Lego block on which the switch should be mounted. This could then be attached temporarily to the front or top of the vehicle.

Research

A simple piece of guided research to help children solve this problem might be as follows. Ask the children to make two foil-covered rectangles of springy plastic and fit them into the crocodile clips from their circuit, as shown in figure 19.

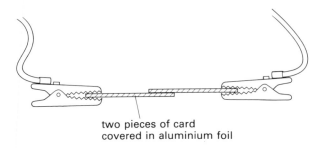

two pieces of card
covered in aluminium foil

Figure 19 Attaching crocodile clips to the pieces of foil-covered card

The bulb will, of course, light up since the foil pieces are in contact. Ask the children to find a way of turning the bulb off by lowering a 20 gram mass on to the strips. (The mass could be covered in sticky tape so that it is a non-conductor or insulator). The mass represents the pressure of the vehicle against the wall.

Possible solutions

Some solutions that will work are illustrated in figure 20.

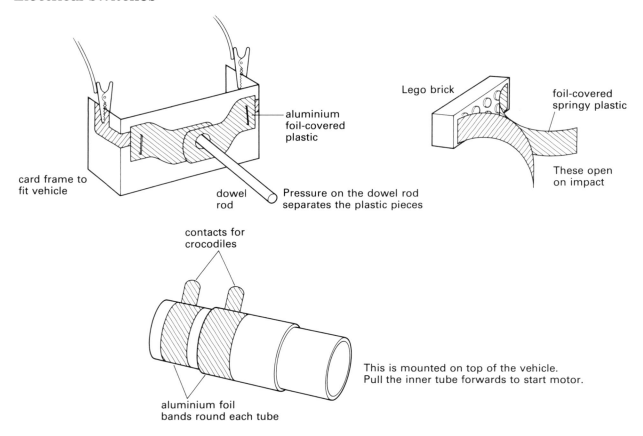

Figure 20 Three designs of pressure switch

Similar projects

Switches can be made for a wide variety of purposes. The mechanics must be fairly simple for children at this stage in their development. Examples of suitable tasks involving switches are:

Design a switch that is operated by a strong wind. In the classroom the wind might be a hair dryer or someone blowing hard.

Design a switch for a torch that comes on when the torch is picked up and goes off when it is put down.

On the theme of burglar alarms, the following would be suitable:

Design a switch that is operated by a trip wire.

Design a switch that comes on when someone stands on a mat.

The following task might be suitable for a switch which can be used in a game of skill:

Design a switch that operates an alarm if an object or a games board is tilted from the horizontal.

Children could have great fun trying to carry such a board around the classroom without tilting it. Of course, the batteries and bulb would have to be built into the board.

7 Folding chairs

THE TASK

Imagine you have a small bedroom but you would like to have friends to visit you there. What you need is a comfortable seat for a friend that can be packed up and stored away when not in use. Your task is to design an attractive chair that can fold up as flat as possible for storage. Using your design drawings you must make a scale model of the chair to one fifth its full size.

Within this project lie many important features of design and construction. Those embarking on it will need to consider the function of their chair and weigh this up carefully against its appearance. Should a chair look good to the detriment of its comfort, or should it be entirely functional to the detriment of aesthetic considerations?

The children will have to consider the needs of people and this will be reflected in their research into bodily proportions. Current practice in the manufacture of furniture could be investigated, as well as the long history of chair-making. Technological principles will be encountered in designing the folding mechanism of the chair and mathematics will emerge as a useful tool in all aspects of the children's work.

A fair degree of competence in handling resistant materials will be required. The use of machine tools such as a bandsaw, pedestal drill and disc sander would be an advantage, though not essential. If such tools are used, a suitable introduction, including safety considerations, must be given to the children. Much can be achieved, however, by using the tools described in this book so far. Wood is the obvious and most adaptable material to use but much is to be gained by introducing children to new materials, such as sheet plastics. These can be cut and shaped in much the same way as wood and would be particularly appropriate in this project. Fabrics must also play an important part in this design exercise since they may be used to cover all or parts of the chair. Separate cushions could be designed for the folding seat and these will need to be sewn and filled with whatever is to hand.

Research

Discuss with the children what form their research should take. There are, as always, a number of possible avenues to follow:

- Find pictures of chair designs, past and present, and note the features that are relevant to the current challenge.
- Write to modern furniture stores for catalogues.
- Look at folding chairs that can be brought into school, such as a deck chair, fishing stool or garden seat.

Figure 1 First step in research

- Conduct a survey to find which style of chair is preferred in a bedroom.
- Visit a furniture shop to make notes on chair design.

Making a model person

An important part of the initial research will be to decide the correct proportions for the chair and this will involve considering the person who will sit on it. We will need to think about the height of the seat above the ground, the angle of the back, and whether to have arm rests or not. In order to do this, we need a model of an average person to work with and this will provide the children with the first exercise in their preparations.

Measuring up

Show the children how they can make a simple model of a person that will later be used to design the chair. A sketch on the blackboard will be sufficient (figure 2).

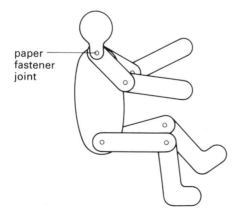

paper
fastener
joint

Figure 2 Jointed designer's model

How will the lengths of various parts of the model's body be decided?

Since the chair will be for a person the same age as the children, we need to have an idea of the average size of such a child. If the group is taken as a representative sample, then, the measurements can be based on the average for the group.

Ask the children to work with a partner to find the lengths in centimetres of the parts of the body shown in the diagram. They can record the results on a sketch of their own. They will have to use commonsense in deciding where the joints begin and end since we have simplified the human form so much.

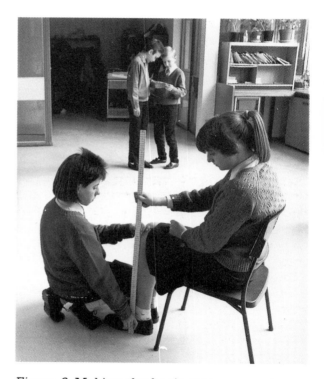

Figure 3 Making the basic measurements

If the results for the whole group are written on the blackboard diagram, then an average for these can be found. This could either be done in a true mathematical sense, i.e. by adding all the values and dividing the total by the number of results, or an approximate value could be obtained by group consensus.

Finally, the full-size measurements must be scaled down to one fifth to match the scale of the model chair. The measurements obtained might be something like those shown in figure 4, though slight variations on this would not be out of place.

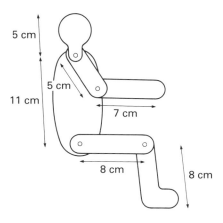

Figure 4 Scaled-down measurements

Putting the model together

The model can be made from card using a hole
punch to cut clean holes for the joints. The
children could be expected to draw their own
simplified limb shapes but they must
remember to make their measurements from
hole centre to hole centre and therefore to cut
the limbs a little longer to allow for this.

Design considerations

Before the children use their model to draw
their chair designs, they will need to consider
the limitations they will be working under
when making their chair.

Show them the materials available for
construction: plywood, hardboard, softwood,
dowel, wire, plastics, fabrics, nails, screws,
hinges, eye hooks, etc.

Discuss various methods for making hinges,
but encourage the children to think of some of
their own. You may decide to have a few hinge
devices (figure 5) on hand to show the children.

Of course, the chair need not necessarily fold
flat with the use of hinges. It could be
dismantled and then packed away flat. Perhaps
the parts could slot together and pull apart.

Appearance

An important feature of this project could be
the final appearance of the model. Show the
children pictures of modern furniture and
encourage some of them to be experimental in
their designs. They could plan to use paint on
parts of their model or settle for a wood finish,
perhaps using a wood stain before varnishing.

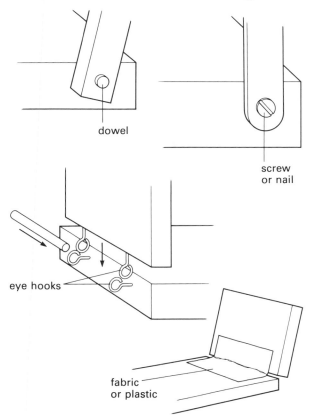

Figure 5 Some ideas for hinges

If the model is to be covered in fabric, they
should plan to paint or varnish the wood before
attaching it.

Design drawings

The children will now be able to appreciate
why they have created a card model. If they
place it in the centre of a large sheet of drawing
paper in a comfortable sitting position, they
can draw around it in preparation for designing
their chair (figure 6). The chair they choose to

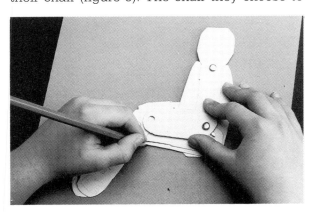

Figure 6 Drawing a comfortably seated person

Folding chairs

make must now be drawn to fit the person sitting in it. This first drawing will be a side view and should show how the hinge will operate if there is to be one. If there are arm rests that would normally obscure the person, these can be drawn ghost-like over the figure. Colour schemes and fabric covering can now be considered and if possible a scrap of fabric could be attached to the drawing.

Further drawing skills

If you consider it appropriate, you could introduce the idea of a more realistic drawing of the chair by showing the children how to draw in oblique projection. The following notes show how this may be done for the chair.

Making an oblique projection

This is sometimes described as a cabinet drawing. Its merit lies in the fact that the front of the model is drawn to its true shape.

Start with a block of wood. It will look like figure 7. Notice that all the vertical lines are drawn vertically on the paper. The front of the block is drawn as its true shape (a rectangle). Lines going away from you are drawn half length and at an angle of 45° to the horizontal.

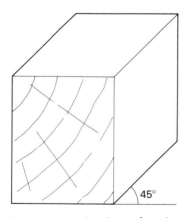

Figure 7 Oblique projection of a simple block

Within this drawing of a cuboid a more complicated shape can be drawn. If we imagine the cuboid is the same height, width and length as the chair we want to draw, then the chair can be 'fitted in' as shown in figure 8.

Drawing a chair in oblique projection

Children can draw their chair by first drawing a cuboid in faint pencil lines, then filling in the chair details in bold pencil. Squared paper will

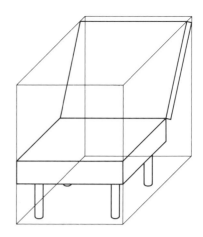

Figure 8 Oblique projection of a chair: front view

be very useful in that lines at 45° can be drawn along the diagonals of the squares. If plain paper is used, a 45° set square will be necessary.

It is worth noting that the side view the children have already drawn will appear on the (distorted) side of the cuboid in the manner adopted above. However, it may be desirable when drawing objects such as chairs to have the side view at the front, as illustrated in figure 9.

Not all of the children in a mixed ability group will find this task easy. If there is time, children could be given a series of simpler drawing tasks before they attempt to draw their chair.

A note about another method of drawing models in a realistic way is made at the end of this chapter.

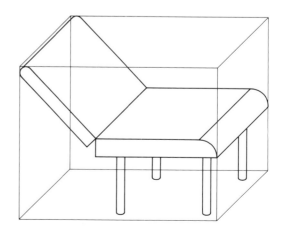

Figure 9 Oblique projection of a chair: side view

Construction

The range of materials you present to the children will be reflected in the variety of models they make. Try to provide a selection of different-sized dowel and small rectangular sections for legs, and sheets of hardboard and plywood cut to convenient sizes.

The following typical situations illustrate some of the ideas that children may have and some of the problems they may have to solve.

Figure 10 Assembling a hinged-back chair

Sally and Melanie's 'legless' chair

Sally and Melanie wanted to avoid the problem of fixing legs to their chair and had decided to use a solid wooden block, suitably padded, for their base. The chair back was to fold up into position and be supported by a swivelling bracket (figure 11).

The back piece was to be hinged with a stiff piece of leather glued to both base and back. The seat was to be padded with foam and covered in fabric. Their teacher suggested that they use a block of dark hardwood for the base

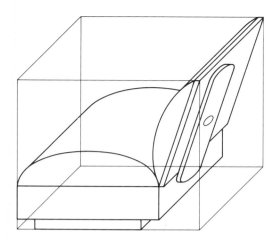

Figure 11 Sally and Melanie's chair

as this was perhaps more attractive and unusual than softwood. The block was then cut to size on a bandsaw to save valuable time.

Jamie's adapted fishing stool

Jamie wanted to use the fishing stool idea but to incorporate a back to lean on. This had led to a complicated and unworkable drawing that was simplified with the help of his teacher (figure 12).

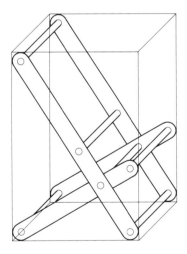

Figure 12 Jamie's chair

John and Dannie's folding chair

John was working with Dannie on a fairly conventional four-legged chair with a folding back. The dowel legs would be plugged into the base but the back would swing down on a dowel pivot (figure 13).

Figure 13 John and Dannie's chair

Sarah's slot-together chair

Sarah had chosen to use coloured plastic and to
make a slot-together chair. The plastic pieces
were slotted into the wooden arms of the chair.
This clever arrangement was not arrived at,
however, on the first attempt. Sarah's first
drawings had the germ of the idea but the
details needed working out. After a discussion
with her teacher, she decided first to make a
card model of the chair to see if it would slot
together successfully (figure 14).

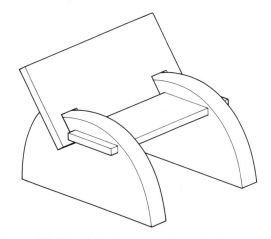

Figure 14 Sarah's slot-together chair

Carol and Susan's fold-away lounger

Carol and Susan worked together on a simple
fold-away lounger. They used hardboard
covered in a striped fabric which doubled as
the hinge material too. The legs were short
blocks of wood that didn't really need folding
away (figure 15).

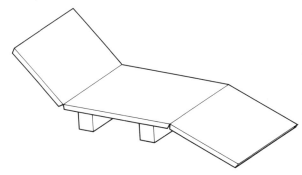

Figure 15 Carol and Susan's lounger

Jason's balloon chair

Jason's plan was to use a balloon to blow his
seat into position, and which at the same time
acted as a cushion. The balloon would need to
be contained somehow and there would need
to be a method for preventing air loss. Jason
was provided with a tube clamp from the
science equipment and he went to work on the
other technical problems (figure 16).

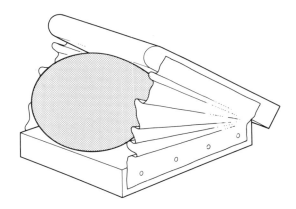

Figure 16 Jason's balloon chair

Lisa and Karla's chair

Lisa and Karla's chair seemed to be a disaster
at first. They had considered carefully the
problem of folding. They had simplified the leg
design by using rectangular sheets of plywood
on each side of the seat but to their dismay the
whole thing folded too easily. In fact it would
not stand up! Their teacher had seen the
problem coming but had let the girls run into
trouble before lending a helping hand. He
knew the problem was not beyond solution and
he knew the girls would not be totally discouraged
at this point.

He let the girls suggest a solution to the
problem of the folding legs (figure 17).

Because their teacher didn't discourage

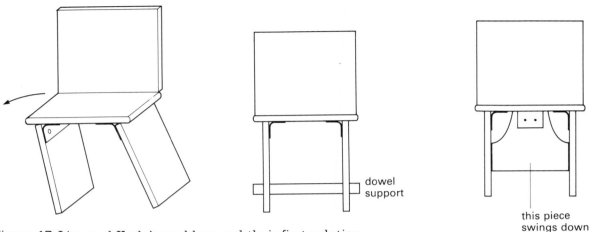

Figure 17 Lisa and Karla's problem and their first solution

them, they were both ready to rush off and try their solution but he stopped them and suggested that there could be other solutions that were worth thinking about.

They sketched some more ideas (figure 18). Eventually the girls chose the wire support idea and realised that their first idea had perhaps not been the best.

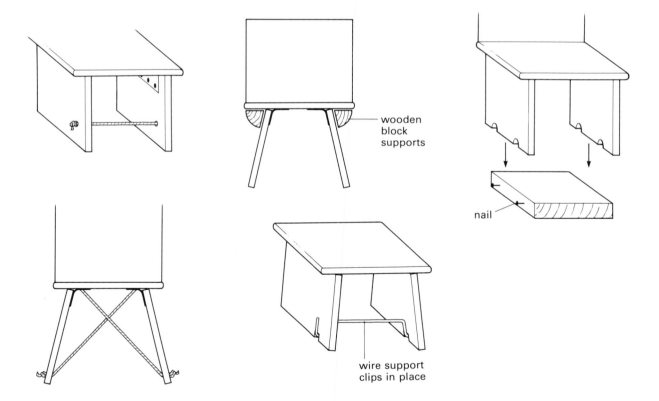

Figure 18 Lisa and Karla's subsequent proposals

Finishing

The following points should be noted if the finished models are to be really well made.

• The chair should be symmetrical in that both sides should match in size and shape.

• All pieces of exposed wood should be sanded smooth before they are fixed together. The final sanding should be made with a fine grade of glasspaper.

Folding chairs

- Any treatment of wooden parts such as paint, wood stain, linseed oil or polyurethane varnish should be applied before the fabric covering is fitted. A glossier finish can be obtained if the first coat of varnish is lightly sanded before the second coat is applied.

- All nails, drawing pins and staples should be hidden from view unless they are purposely designed to enhance the appearance of the model.

Display and evaluation

When all the models are finished, they should be to the same scale so they can be displayed as though they are in a furniture shop with the original card models seated in them.

The children will have been continually evaluating their models as work has progressed, but it might be worth reminding them of the original brief to see how far they have actually fulfilled it:

- Does the chair look attractive?

- Does it look comfortable to sit in and does the model fit comfortably in it?

- How flat will it fold up?

- Would you use one in your bedroom?

Similar projects

Projects where an elementary study of ergonomics and scale are involved are as follows:

Design a settee that could fold into a bed.

Design a piece of playground apparatus suitable for eight-year-olds. Your model should include at least one moving part. Consider the safety aspects for young children.

Design a single bed that can double as a work table for a small bedroom

Design a three-wheeled fun vehicle for a toddler than can be made in wood.

Design a table than can fold to half its size.

In each design project, card models of an average-sized grown-up could be made. In the case of a child's toy, could the appropriate measurements be obtained from a local infant school or a playgroup?

Finding out what is already on the market is an important part of manufacturing research. Magazines and catalogues can usually be obtained from home or by writing for them. In many cases, real objects can be brought into the classroom to aid further study.

Figure 19 Five contrasting designs

ABOUT . . .

Design drawings

Besides the oblique projection described earlier, a similar method which gives a realistic view of model is the isometric projection. Teachers might like to introduce this to their children as an effective means of illustration.

Isometric projection

A housebrick might be drawn like this in isometric projection.

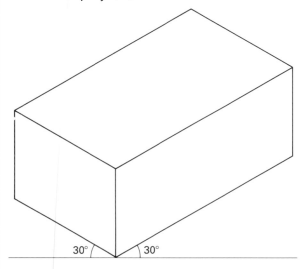

Notice that all vertical lines are drawn vertically while all horizontal lines are drawn at 30 degrees to the horizontal.

Shapes which fit neatly into a cuboid can be drawn by sketching the cuboid in faint pencil first then completing the drawing in bolder pencil.

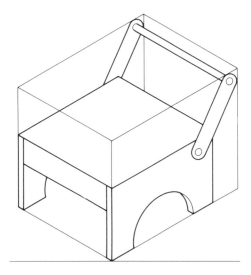

Notice that both side views of the chair are distorted.

8 Children's problems

This final chapter is concerned with children who find and solve problems of their choice. The motivating influence on children following their own interests is well known and makes sense. The reality, however, is often very different from the desired situation with the limited time, resources and facilities available in schools. So the following pages try to capture a typical situation within the restrictions of the school environment.

The starting point is a group of children who have had experience in solving specific problems, similar to those already described in this book. It is assumed that they have learnt how to use tools correctly and safely and have a working knowledge of the materials available to them. More important is the children's experience in working through the complete design process. They know the different forms that initial research can take. They appreciate the different ways of planning their designs from simple sketch to card modelling. They are prepared to analyse a temporary problem and consider solutions that are appropriate to it, and they have learnt to have confidence in their ability to win through in the end.

Any of the children's problems described here could be taken as a project for a whole group to solve and perhaps, initially, you would like to use these ideas in this way. This might then lead the children to suggest more school-based problems to solve in a later project.

Introduction

Mrs Herbert taught in the fourth year at Raycott School, so when she came to take a group of children for design and technology in the summer term she knew them well enough to try the following project. She wanted to open up the idea of problem solving and get them to find problems of their own. She realised that tackling the initial part of the problem-solving process – finding and defining a problem – was not easy but she felt the children were ready for it. Many problems, of course, are not easily solved within the confines of a classroom or workshop, and some solutions do not require a device to be made, so these would not be appropriate. Nevertheless, Mrs Herbert decided to talk to the group of children to see what ideas they had.

She decided to restrict the problem-solving projects to ones in the school environment. She managed to meet the group for a short time before the design and technology lesson and asked them to think about and note down difficulties and problems that they had noticed around school ready for their first lesson with her.

When they next met she divided the school into physical areas and asked the children to think about each area, its problems, and where improvements could be made. She began with a problem of her own to set the scene.

She told the children of her difficulty in carrying books and equipment from one part of the school to another. Often she had a pile of books to carry and a box of scissors and a tin of crayons and sometimes she needed glue pots with spreaders. Sometimes she could ask someone to help her but at other times it might take her two trips.

Eventually she solved the problem by bringing a shopping bag trolley from home and fixing a strong box to it. At the same time she found she had also solved the problem of carrying things to and from her car at the beginning and end of school.

The trolley worked well until one day she had to carry her load up steps to a classroom. She now realised she had another problem to be solved.

'I don't expect you to solve my problem for me, but what other kinds of problems have you noticed around school? Think of those in your classroom to begin with.'

Melanie began with a complaint that whenever she needed something from her tray, such as a ruler or a new book, it was always difficult to get at it because the classroom seemed so crowded. She had tried to solve this problem by putting her tray on her desk, but had then found that there wasn't enough room to work.

Dannie joined in to explain that his felt pens were always rolling off his desk and getting lost, and whenever Jamie couldn't find his pencil sharpener he came over and borrowed Dannie's

'We need proper places to keep these things,' he said.

Lisa explained that she kept things in her bag on the floor but that it was difficult to find those things that had slipped to the bottom.

Mrs Herbert was anxious to keep the discussion away from the solution of specific problems for the moment, so she suggested that they consider the playground as a possible source of problems.

Sarah had noticed the wind blowing paper out of a full waste bin in the corner of the playground.

'The younger children are untidy enough with their litter without the wind helping them,' she complained.

'I wish we had somewhere to sit at playtime. It's all right in the summer when we are allowed on the grass but not in spring and autumn.'

Sabrina was stating a wish shared by many in the group.

Karla remembered when there used to be a bar to swing on at the top of the playground. She wondered if they could have something to replace the one that was taken away. Others in the group agreed that some sort of playground apparatus would be great fun.

Gradually Mrs Herbert and her group talked through problems concerning each part of the school. They discussed the corridors, the hall and the entrance. They imagined they were visitors to the school and talked about finding their way around a strange building. They discussed playtimes and lunchtimes – especially wet ones. A lively discussion centred on what there was to do during wet playtimes and how the situation could be improved.

Defining the problem

Finally Mrs Herbert asked her group to think about a problem they would like to solve within the school environment. The problem should be one for which a device or a scale model would be needed.

She asked each child to write down clearly the problem they were going to solve, and then to make a series of doodles to illustrate some possible solutions. If a problem required a number of devices or models, then they could work in a team of not more than three or four.

The desk tidy

Both Peter and John had sympathised with Dannie when he had explained about his pens falling off the desk. Peter wrote this:

Things like my pens and rubbers are always getting knocked from my desk and sometimes I lose my pencil sharpener or pair of compasses under my books. I want something to keep all these things in and it must have my name on so that people know it is mine.

The things I want to keep in my holder are felt pens, pencil sharpener, paperclips, compasses, football stickers, rubber, pad of paper.

Research

I checked in some shops at the weekend to see what was on sale. I made some drawings from a stationery catalogue Mrs Herbert gave me.

I measured my pens to see what size tube I need.

I measured 30 of my football stickers to make sure they will fit in a box.

Some solutions

Peter's design drawings are shown in figure 1.

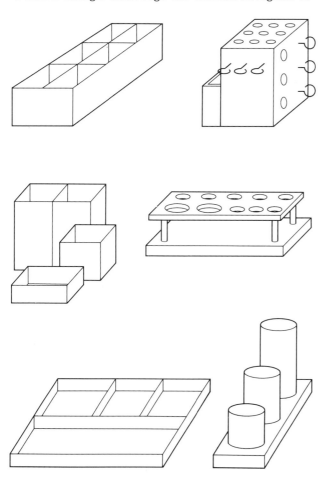

Figure 1 Variety of designs for the desk tidy

Peter went on to make his holder on a wooden base. He made use of some plastic tubing that Mrs Herbert offered him and fixed this with an epoxy resin for greater strength.

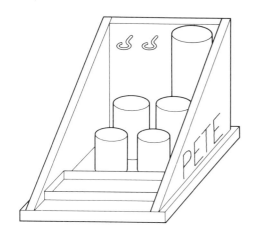

Figure 2 Peter's holder

John's tidybox (figure 3) was quite different, although it served the same purpose. He was determined to clamp his to the edge of the desk, so he brought a simple metal clamp from home and built this into his box.

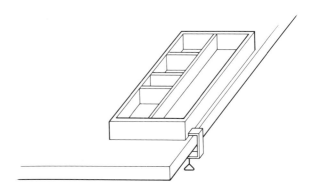

Figure 3 John's tidybox

The new desk

Melanie decided that she would solve the crowded desk problem by completely redesigning the desk. This was how she stated her problem:

My problem is that I would like all the things I need for my work to be there ready when I want them. I would like a place for my writing things, my books, and my project folder. I would like to have my bag by my desk too. When I go out to play I change into my pumps so I would like a place for my shoes. Not in my desk because they are smelly!

Research

I asked my mum and dad what kind of desk they had when they were at school. My dad made a drawing for me.

I looked in a catalogue at office desks.

I measured my desk and tray and tried to estimate how much storage space I need.

I will make a scale model one-quarter the size of the desk I would like.

First ideas

Melanie's initial designs are shown in figure 4.

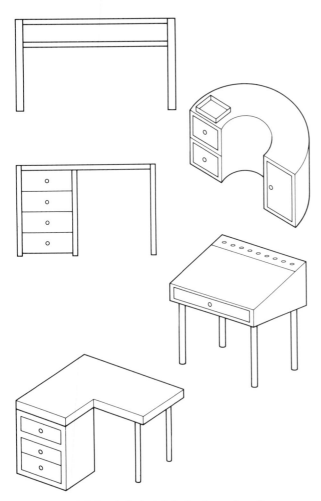

Figure 4 Melanie's initial designs for the new desk

Melanie used hardboard pieces and short lengths of beading to make her finished model. The drawers were made from cardboard.

Figure 5 Melanie's improved desk

The display surfaces

Lisa and Sally had overheard a teacher saying that the school needed some display shelving for three-dimensional objects. They decided to work together to make a model of a display rack for a vertical wall. They wrote:

We would like to make some shelves for the wall.

Mrs Herbert explained that this was a solution to a problem, not the problem itself, and asked them to rewrite their problem clearly.

The display problem

The problem is there are no safe places to show things like pottery or models in the school. Ordinary shelves in rows are so boring and the tables outside the classroom are always being knocked into. We will make some display surfaces that are attractive themselves.

Research

We must look at the display surfaces in school already. We must also talk to the caretaker to see if she has any in store.

We will look round furniture stores to see the shelving that is available.

Some solutions

Some of the solutions Lisa and Sally considered are shown in figure 6.

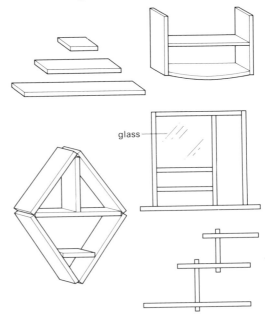

glass

Figure 6 Lisa and Sally's ideas for display surfaces

The final design drawing

Finally they settled for the design in figure 7.

We will make a model one-sixth the full size and fix it in a cardboard box 'room'.

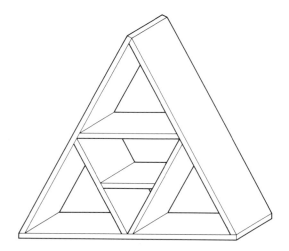

Figure 7 Lisa and Sally's final design drawing

The roll-a-penny game

Karla and Sabrina wrote:

When we have to stay in at playtime or lunchtime because it is wet, it can get very boring with nothing to do. We need some interesting games to play.

Although it was they who were 'bored' at playtime, the girls decided to make a game suitable to the first years to play.

Research

We will make a questionnaire to find out what kind of board games children like playing.

We will also read books about Victorian games to get some unusual ideas and look in toy catalogues.

During their research, the girls redefined their task so that in the end they decided to make a game based on rolling a penny on to a board. The game could still be used at playtime with counters, but it would have the dual purpose of being available at school fairs and other events.

Additional research

We will play with different kinds of slope for the coin to roll down, and try different coins.

Some solutions for the slope and target board

These are illustrated in figures 8 and 9 respectively. The girls went on to make their own version of roll-a-penny to fit exactly on a school desk.

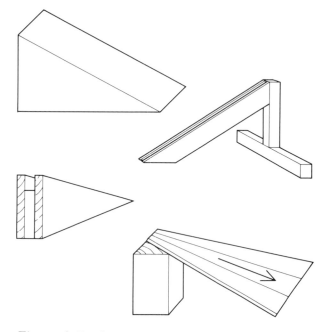

Figure 8 Designs for the roll-a-penny slope

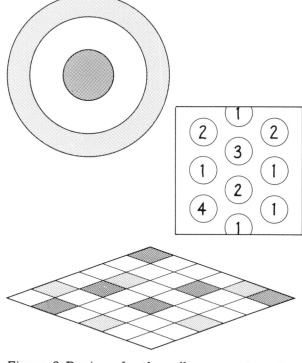

Figure 9 Designs for the roll-a-penny target board

Playground apparatus

Sarah and Carol had found that Stephen and Martin were working on the same problem, although they had worded it in slightly different ways. Sarah had written:

At playtime some children like to play on apparatus like we have in the gym. They like to climb or swing or perhaps jump. We need something that allows us to do these things. The thing we build should be good to look at as well as fun to play on.

The four of them decided to work as a team and make a complete set of playground apparatus.

Research

This was how they defined their research programme:

Find out what children want.

Make a list of all the activities that children could do at playtime like jumping, sliding and swinging.

Look at local playgrounds for ideas.

Make card models of some apparatus to see what they looks like.

Make a card model of a child to get the right sizes for the apparatus.

Some solutions

They sketched the four ideas shown in figure 10.

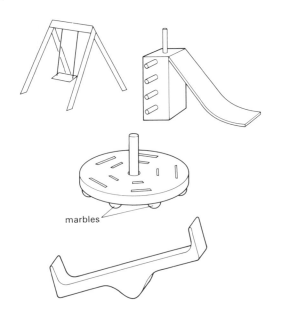

Figure 10 Different types of playground apparatus

Eventually Martin made a wooden slide, Sarah made a climbing frame, and Carol and Stephen both made a roundabout. They had agreed on a scale of 1:4 for their models and displayed them on a card plan of their real playground.

The shoe cleaner

Susan and Dannie had noticed a problem that had not come up in the first discussion and they set out to solve it in their project.

On a rainy day when we have been outside to play, some children walk on the muddy bits by the side of the path and when they come into school the mud comes off on the carpets. Sometimes when there is a check on muddy shoes the children are sent outside to clean them but there is nowhere that this can be done. We think there should be a shoe cleaning machine for us to clean our shoes before they are checked.

Research

They further noted:

Get some different shoes and make them dirty by putting mud on them. See how difficult it is to clean it off using a cloth, a sponge, a brush.

Find out if water will help. Do we need soap? How much will that cost?

Some solutions

Four of Susan and Dannie's proposals are illustrated in figure 11.

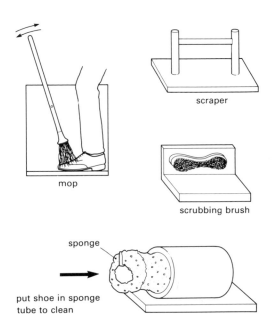

scraper

scrubbing brush

sponge

put shoe in sponge tube to clean

Figure 11 Ideas for the shoe cleaner

Design drawing for the shoe cleaner

They finally settled for the design in figure 12, and explained:

The watering can is there to put a little water and soap on the brushes (with the shoe out of the way).

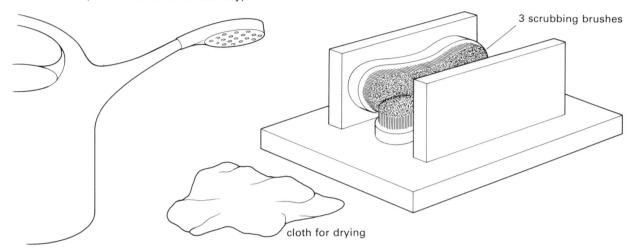

3 scrubbing brushes

cloth for drying

Figure 12 Final design for the shoe cleaner

The wellie remover

Jason had always had trouble with getting his wellies off. This happened at home when he came in from play and at school when his class came back from a recent field trip. He decided to look into the problem:

When you have to take wellies off and they are muddy or slippery, it is very difficult especially if your wellies are too small for you. The school needs something that will help everyone take their wellies off at the end of a trip.

Research

Jason had two things to research:

Find out the range of sizes of wellies used in school. Measure the length and width of these wellies.

Find out how others have made wellie removers.

The problem

The wellie remover must grip the bottom of the wellie and stay on the ground so that you can lift your foot out. If there is something to hold on to when you do this, it would be easier.

Some solutions

Jason's first solutions are shown in figure 13.

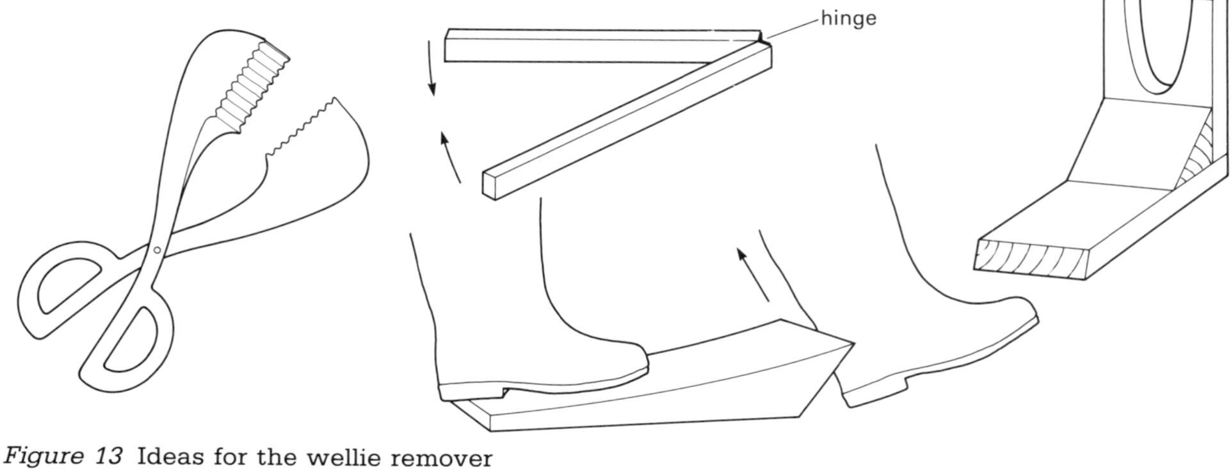

hinge

Figure 13 Ideas for the wellie remover

The final design

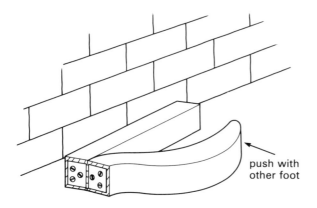

Figure 14 Final design for the wellie remover

In fact figure 14 wasn't Jason's final design. When he had finished making his wellie remover he found it difficult to keep it on the ground while the foot was pulled up. He carried out a number of trials before he worked out what to do. He decided the answer was to fix it securely to a large baseboard which the user could stand on, thus holding the whole contraption on the ground.

The final, final solution

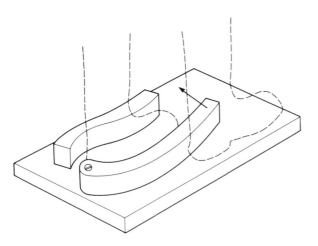

Figure 15 Jason's improved final design for the wellie remover

The waste bin

David and Jamie could not decide which problem to tackle, so Mrs Herbert asked them to look into the problem of litter being blown from the waste bin in the playground. At first the two boys were reluctant to tackle this, but once they had started discussing it with their teacher it became more and more interesting.

When the bin in the playground gets full of paper, the wind blows the top layer out over the playground and we have to go and pick it up again. It isn't very nice squashing the papers down in the bin again so we would like to stop this happening.

Some ideas for solutions

David and Jamie listed their ideas:

Stop children eating sweets and crisps in the playground at break and lunch times.

Put the bin in a sheltered place. This would have to be in the building.

Put a heavy weight on the papers in the bin. This would make it difficult to get litter in!

Design a bin with a very thin neck so that the paper can't escape.

Make a bin with a lid.

Make a lid for the existing bin.

The two boys decided to concentrate on making a model of a better shaped bin with a lid.

We want to make it easy to get litter into the bin.

Research

We will look at pedal bins that you get in kitchens.

We will look at swing lid bins.

We will think about different materials with which to make the bin and lid.

Materials

David and Jamie listed materials which could be used:

Metal – galvanised iron, aluminium

Wood – rustic log effect, stained softwood

Plastic

Some solutions

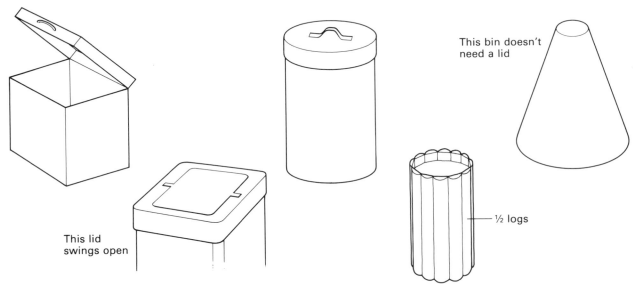

Figure 16 Waste bin designs

Eventually the boys chose to have a plastic liner in the bin so that it could be easily emptied. They also decided to have a log effect exterior for good looks.

David decided to work on a model of the bin while Jamie experimented with a lid that would open easily and keep the litter in. Their final solution was built to a scale 1:4.

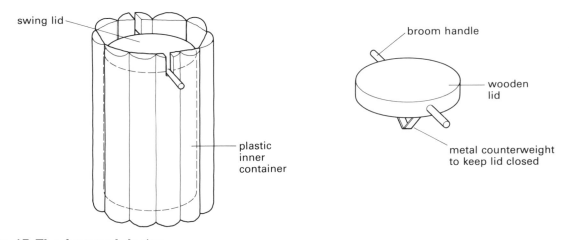

Figure 17 The favoured design

Concluding remarks

At the end of the project, Mrs Herbert gathered the children in her group around to tell them how pleased she was that they had attempted to solve so many problems in and around the school. The children who had been working so hard on their own projects were interested to hear what the others in the group had been doing. Not all the models were complete and not all the problems were completely solved in the fixed time that had been given. Some

children were taking their plans home to continue working in the summer holiday and they promised to bring their efforts back to show their teacher.

Each child had a project folder that he/she had filled with notes and diagrams as the project went along. These folders, with the models the children had made, were put on display for the school open day.

The children left Raycott School at the end of term ready to continue solving practical problems with confidence.

Safety triangles

1 Craft knives

All craft knifes are sharp enough to cut into flesh. Ensure children know what to do if they do happen to cut themselves. Have a first aid box ready in any craft area.

Table surfaces can be protected with a cutting board or a thick magazine or newspaper. Children should have enough control to be able to guide the blade of the knife without it suddenly slipping. The most important safety rule is to keep all parts of the body – especially fingers – out of the path of the blade. Always assume that the blade *might* slip.

2 Rasps and files

A wooden or plastic handle must always be fitted to the tang of a file or rasp before it is used. The handle should be tapped on to ensure a tight fit. Without a handle, the tang could be driven into the hand if the file or rasp catches on the work.

3 Hot glue gun

A hot glue gun works by melting a stick of adhesive as it is pushed through an electrical heater in the gun. Because it is electrical, it should be kept away from any source of water. The melted glue is very hot and can stick to fingers and hands, causing a burn which may blister. Should this happen the burnt area of skin must be placed immediately under running cold water for a couple of minutes.

A special glueing table should be set up away from the general movement in the classroom and children should be given clear instructions on how to use the gun before they begin.

All electrical appliances, such as the hot glue gun, should be kept and used well away from any water.

4 Securing material to be cut

The material could be wood or plastic and the method of cutting could be with a saw or a drill. The material should only be held by hand if it is being held in a bench hook and sawn. Otherwise, use a G-cramp or a vice.

Material to be drilled should always be held in a vice or with a G-cramp, *never* held by hand.

5 Polyurethane varnish

Polyurethane varnish will give an effective finish to some wooden models, but certain precautions should be observed. These are often explained on the container and usually include the following:

- Ensure good ventilation during application and drying.
- Remove splashes from the skin with a recognised cleaner.
- If splashes enter eyes, wash them with plenty of water.
- Store and use away from heat and flame.
- Do not store cloths used for wiping up varnish.

It is usually advisable to limit the number of children using the varnish at any time and insist that they wear protective clothing.

The white spirit used to clean the brushes is flammable and may irritate the eyes and skin. The appropriate precautions must be taken.

6 Electrical safety

The difference between the safe electrical current from low-voltage batteries and the dangerous current from the mains must be made clear to children. They should never touch mains appliances without adult supervision.

7 Power drill, band saw, jig saw and sander

These electrical tools may be included in the work area that you are using. Make it clear to children that they are not to use these unless they have permission and have received the correct instruction in how to use them. The manufacturers' instructions must be followed exactly as regards operation and safety precautions.

Safety triangles

Children should not crowd around such tools and must not interfere with those who are operating them. Where necessary, the children should be taught to use safety goggles for certain operations.

8 Eye protection when drilling or sawing

Eyes should be kept well away from the workpiece. Particles are scattered by the action of a drill bit or a saw.

9 Wallpaper paste

Never use fungicidal wallpaper paste. It is poisonous. Also children should be warned of the dangers of placing non-fungicidal wallpaper paste anywhere near their mouths. Hands should be washed thoroughly after use.

Index